THE FUNDAMENTALS OF **GUARDIANSHIP**

What Every Guardian Should Know

Cover design by Tahiti Spears/ABA Design

Printed in the United States of America.

22 21 20 7 6 5

ISBN: 978-1-63425-721-3
e-ISBN: 978-1-63425-722-0

Library of Congress Cataloging-in-Publication Data

Title: Fundamentals of guardianship : what every guardian should know
Description: Chicago : American Bar Association, 2017.
Identifiers: LCCN 2016051227 (print) | LCCN 2016051306 (ebook) | ISBN 9781634257213 (softcover : alk. paper) | ISBN 9781634257220 ()
Subjects: LCSH: Guardian and ward—United States.
Classification: LCC KF553 .H87 2017 (print) | LCC KF553 (ebook) | DDC 346.7301/8—dc23
LC record available at https://lccn.loc.gov/2016051227

Discounts are available for books ordered in bulk. Special consideration is given to state bars, CLE programs, and other bar-related organizations. Inquire at Book Publishing, ABA Publishing, American Bar Association, 321 N. Clark Street, Chicago, Illinois 60654-7598.

www.shopABA.org

CONTENTS

INTRODUCTION

The **mission** of the **National Guardianship Association** is to advance the nationally recognized standard of excellence in guardianship.
The **vision** of the **National Guardianship Association** is every person will be provided respect, due process, rights, and dignity in guardianship.

Purpose

Although each state has developed its own procedures for initiating and administering guardianships and conservatorships, the National Guardianship Association (NGA) developed this book primarily to provide general information to family, professional, and public guardians and conservators so that they are able to provide services that would meet or exceed all state requirements.

NGA hopes that anyone involved with or interested in the well-being of persons facing or **under guardianship** will benefit from having access to this concise book describing the fundamental responsibilities of a guardian.

NGA, founded in 1988 as a nonprofit national organization, strives to strengthen the practice of guardianship and related services through networking and education. NGA believes that the practice of guardianship should always be conducted in the most professional and ethical manner and that nationally recognized standards of excellence in guardianship should be encouraged and promoted.

Many NGA members are not guardians, but work in a collateral capacity with guardians. Active members include professional care managers, social workers, attorneys, educators, court administrators, judges, and other community professionals involved in guardianships, but not acting as guardians themselves.

Standards and Ethics

NGA has adopted **standards of practice** that reflect a high quality of performance in addition to **Ethical Principles** that address the relationship between a guardian and a person subject to guardianship. The first ten standards were developed in 1991 and expanded in 2000 to twenty-five. Additional revisions were added in 2002, 2007, and again in 2013 to reflect advances in guardianship practices.

Please refer to both the **NGA Standards of Practice** and the Ethical Principles (both available at www.guardianship.org) included in this book. Throughout this book are references to the relevant NGA Standards of Practice.

Certification

The Center for Guardianship Certification (CGC) is a nonprofit organization that provides a comprehensive guardianship certification program to encourage, support, and foster best practices for quality guardianship services. The qualifications for the CGC's certification programs are often more stringent than state requirements. Achieving the National Certified Guardian (NCG) credential demonstrates that an individual possesses basic knowledge and understanding of guardianship, its governing ethical principles and practice standards. To obtain CGC's highest credential, National Master Guardian (NMG), a person must meet high qualifications and pass a day-long examination covering more advanced concepts and specialized topics. CGC certification is available in all states for all guardians, with some states requiring either CGC or state certification for specific types of guardians.

Certification alone does not guarantee that the individual will properly perform the duties and responsibilities of a guardian or act in accordance with all state laws. It is, however, NGA's and CGC's mutual goal to ensure that individuals are properly prepared to fulfill their obligations as guardians (Standard 1.II).

Glossary

A tremendous variety of terms are currently in use in the guardianship field. Some are legally defined; many are specific to a particular state. To help the reader understand the terminology used in this book, the authors provide a glossary. The first time a term defined in the glossary is used or discussed in the text it is highlighted in **bold**.

ACKNOWLEDGMENTS

The first version of the Fundamentals of Guardianship, developed by Greg Mullowney and Francine Saccio, was published by the National Guardianship Association in 2001. In 2004 NGA's Training and Education Committee took this text framework, redesigned the material, added references to the Standards of Practice, and developed resources and a glossary. The dedicated persons on this subcommittee were Chairperson Vickie V. Alkire, Sally Hurme, Beth Upshaw Mathews, and Susan McMahon. In 2014, the NGA Education Committee under the leadership of Chairperson Helen Ferraro-Zaffram and the work of the committee members Ginny Casazza, Lauren Sherman, and Sally Hurme made major revisions to reflect the evolution of guardianship practice and NGA's updated Standards of Practice.

A very special thank you to those who have contributed their valuable time, energy, and expertise to this project over the years.

1

Guardianship and Its Alternatives

Overview of Guardianship

Each state has developed its own legal criteria and process for determining when an individual is legally incapacitated and, as a result of this **incapacity**, is unable to make decisions to care for his or her personal matters or property. Depending on state terminology, the **court** appoints an individual or entity to serve as **guardian** or **conservator**. For clarity, because of the various terms used in the states, the term "guardianship" throughout this book includes the appointment of a surrogate decision maker for either personal or financial matters. A reference to a guardian includes a conservator and all other types of guardians, except where indicated.

It is important to note that the terms "disability," "incapacity," and "**incompetence**" are not intended to be attached to any particular category of people. However, the three major categories of adults who often need to have a guardian appointed are those who lack decision-making capacity due to **dementia**, those who have an **intellectual disability,** and those who have a mental illness. Others who may require a guardian are individuals who have a brain injury or physical trauma that causes the individual to have diminished **capacity** to make decisions or communicate them in a clear manner.

Another note on terminology: the current trend is moving away from using the term "ward" to refer to a person for whom the court has appointed a guardian. While it is has been used historically, the term has derogatory connotations and to many individuals it is truly an unfavorable four-letter word. In keeping with the current usage, the authors use "person," "client," "adult," or "individual."

In all cases, guardians should keep in mind the following points:

- All adults are presumed to be **competent** until a court proceeding determines otherwise.
- Guardianships are established only through a legal process and are subject to court supervision (Standard 2).
- Incapacity is a legal definition, which must be based upon a mental or medical assessment along with other evidence of the individual's lack of decision-making abilities.
- All guardianships should be based on the actual decision-making ability of the individual without regard to the mental or medical diagnosis.

- Because guardianship removes many of the individual's civil rights, ways to avoid removing those rights must be explored before a guardian is appointed.
- Every guardianship should be designed and limited to meet the individual's needs.
- The guardian must at all times treat the individual with dignity (Standard 3.I).

Types of Guardianship

In general, states authorize the courts to appoint a guardian of the person, a guardian of the estate (which in some states is called a conservator), or a **plenary guardian** with full authority to make all decisions for both the person and the estate. Other types of guardianship are **limited guardianships** or emergency (or temporary) guardianships.

State statutes specify the types of guardianship that a court may order. It is the guardian's responsibility to know the types of guardianship available and the specific authority that can be granted to guardians under each type of guardianship in their state (Standard 2.I).

A **guardian of the person** has the authority only to make decisions relating to the personal, nonfinancial affairs of the person under guardianship. These decisions may include where the person resides and what types of medical, psychological, and psychiatric treatment the person is to receive. Many states require specific court approval for intrusive treatments such as electroconvulsive therapy (ECT) and prohibit treatment that violates the person's known objections. The guardian of the person is responsible for knowing the applicable state statutes and limitations on his or her authority (Standard 2.I).

A **guardian of the estate** is granted the authority only to make decisions relating to the property and finances of the person. These decisions may concern debt payments, asset liquidation, investment management, real estate transactions, and personal finances. Many states require specific court approval for the guardian to engage in certain financial transactions, such as the sale of the home. The guardian of the estate is responsible for knowing the applicable statutory criteria for conducting all financial transactions on behalf of the person (Standard 2.I).

Although it may be necessary to remove all of an individual's rights and grant total responsibility to a guardian, guardianships should be limited to the needs of the person. Courts should allow the person to keep decision-making responsibility in areas where he or she has the ability to make and communicate informed decisions. An individual, for example, may not be able to understand the need to see a doctor or take medicines, but he or she may be able to safely remain at home and carefully manage personal finances. In such cases, the court may find it appropriate to grant only medical decision-making authority to the guardian. As another example, the court may order a medical guardianship, giving the guardian the authority to make only medical decisions for the person. These are often granted for a very specific purpose and limited time, such as 30 or 60 days. Thus, a **limited guardian** receives only those powers specifically designated by the court when it finds that the person remains able to perform some, but not all, of the tasks necessary to care for person or property. Limited guardians possess fewer powers than plenary guardians. Limited guardians are responsible for knowing the limitations of their authority and act consistently with the order (Standard 2.I).

In addition, most states allow for **emergency** or **temporary guardianships**. These time-limited guardianships are intended to provide only the protection needed to respond to an immediate crisis. Again, guardians should be familiar with state statutes that limit the time in which they may make decisions. They should also be familiar with and have a copy of the court's written order. The order will specify the limited decision areas and timeframe in which the temporary guardian may act.

Courts have the responsibility to determine who will be appointed as guardian. Generally, courts prefer to appoint a **family member** as a guardian, but if no family member is available or suitable, courts may look to **professional**, **corporate**, or **public guardians**. Many statutes set forth a list of who should be given priority when selecting among possible guardians, including the person the individual nominated in another document, the agent named in a power of attorney or health care declaration, the guardian appointed in another state, as well as the spouse, adult child, or relative with whom he or she resides. Using the priority list as a guide, judges have the discretion to pick the guardian they believe will best be able to meet the person's needs.

In many cases, the issue is not who to select among several possible candidates, but rather who to appoint when there is no capable or suitable person. Most states have some type of office of public guardian or nonprofit agency that the court appoints as a last resort when there is no other person to serve. The public guardian is an officer of the court or a state employee whose primary function is to provide guardianship services.

Alternatives to Guardianship

Guardianship should be initiated as a last resort. It should be used only when it can be effective and there are no suitable, **less restrictive alternatives**. Serious consideration should be given to ways to avoid guardianship because guardianship results in the removal of the individual's legal rights and restricts the individual's rights to autonomy and self-determination. Developing supportive relationships or finding alternative treatments or an alternative residence can often avoid guardianship (Standard 8.I).

Some alternatives may provide simpler forms of assistance that allow the individual to retain more rights and decision-making responsibilities. These alternatives include obtaining case management services, an **advance directive**, or representative payeeship for Social Security, Supplemental Security Income, Veteran's Administration, or other public benefits.

Advance Directives

The various types of advance directives can be effective tools to avoid guardianships. These include health care powers of attorney, living wills, and financial powers of attorney. The trend in the United States favors the use of advance directives. Prior to appointing a guardian, most courts are required to review any advance directives that an individual prepared prior to becoming incapacitated to determine if the authority outlined in the advance directive meets the person's needs. This approach promotes the use of less restrictive alternatives to guardianship.

However, the court may decline to endorse the authority designated in an advance directive if any of the following criteria are met:

- The individual lacked capacity at the time the advance directive was executed.
- The document does not meet legal requirements.
- The document no longer reflects the individual's wishes.
- The designated decision maker is unable or unwilling to act or is abusing the directive.
- The document was obtained through coercion or undue influence.

Durable Powers of Attorney

Durable power of attorney is a type of advance directive authorized by state statutes. It allows an individual, called the principal, to delegate to another person the authority to become his or her agent and make decisions that the principal is unable to make personally.

A principal may execute a durable power of attorney for health care as well as a durable power of attorney for property management. To be a "durable" power of attorney, the document must specifically state that the principal intends for the agent to act after the principal has become incapacitated. Principals can delegate to the agent whatever powers they wish.

The agent's authority typically begins when the power is signed and always ends when the principal dies. However, the principal may choose a later date or specific event when the power becomes effective. This is called a "springing" power. Most health care powers of attorney are springing. This means that the agent gains the authority to make decisions only after the attending physician has determined that the patient does not have the capacity to make the medical decision.

Any modification or revocation of the power of attorney must be completed according to state law. A court may intervene if it finds that an agent is not acting according to the terms set out in the power of attorney.

Generally, the agent has priority of decision making over a guardian. In some states, however, the appointment of a guardian or conservator overrides the authority of the agent. Because the guardian's authority may be significantly affected by a power of attorney, it is extremely important that the guardian determine whether the person prepared any powers of attorney prior to the guardianship. If the individual recently signed the power of attorney, the court may address concerns that the principal lacked the capacity to execute it. In all cases, guardians should obtain a copy of the power of attorney, make sure the court is aware of the existence of a health care or financial power of attorney, and ensure that all necessary individuals or entities have copies, as appropriate (Standard 14.VI).

Health Care Directives

Competent individuals have the right to consent to or refuse any medical treatment, including life-sustaining treatment. Almost all states have enacted laws that allow individuals, while still capable, to state their wishes in a legal document and to appoint someone to carry out those wishes when they are no longer able to make or communicate medical decisions. These wishes and instructions, known as health care or advance directives, can be in the form of living wills and health care powers of attorney. These documents can provide reliable information to the guardian, the court, and health care providers about the preferences and choices the incapacitated person would make if he or she was capable.

Living Wills

The living will allows terminally ill patients to outline their wishes regarding the use of death-delaying, or life-prolonging, procedures. In living wills, patients may state if they want to refuse or authorize the use of specific medical procedures and outline the circumstances under which death-delaying procedures are to be discontinued. Death-delaying procedures are medical procedures that cannot restore health but serve to prolong or delay the dying process. Examples include mechanical ventilation, kidney dialysis, or tubes to provide food or water. Before these specific procedures can be withheld or withdrawn, at least one physician must certify that the patient has a terminal condition or is in a persistent vegetative state. Treatment or medications for the alleviation of pain are not considered to be life-prolonging treatments. Pain medication, or **palliative care**, will not be withheld if the patient has requested no death-delaying treatments.

Guardians should actively investigate whether the person executed a living will. If one exists, the guardian should ensure that it is followed (Standard 14.VI). This necessitates informing the patient's physician and caregivers of the existence of the living will and closely monitoring the care being provided should the person become terminally ill.

Health Care Power of Attorney

By signing a health care power of attorney, the individual selects a person to make certain that health care preferences are carried out. The health care agent becomes the advocate and spokesperson for the patient when the patient becomes unable to direct his or her own health care. The principal can delegate authority to make other health care decisions in addition to life-sustaining treatments, if desired. In many states, the living will and power of attorney are combined on one form.

Health Care Surrogate Acts

If an advance directive has not been executed, or for some reason does not apply (the court determines it to be invalid for failure to comply with the state law, for example), most state laws provide a way to identify the person who is to make health care decisions, including foregoing life-sustaining treatment, on behalf of the patient.

These health care surrogate laws usually apply to individuals who have a specific health condition and are unable to make decisions about a specific health care matter. These laws provide detailed procedures for the attending physician to follow if the patient lacks the ability to make the decision and has not selected a surrogate decision maker.

Health care surrogate acts typically set forth a list of persons who may serve as the surrogate (sometimes referred to as the proxy) when the incapacitated individual has not previously named someone to make a decision on their behalf. The list prioritizes who may act as surrogate according to the relationship to the individual. The priority list may include the guardian of the person, the spouse, an adult child, a parent, an adult sibling, an adult grandchild, a close friend, or the guardian of the estate. The selected surrogate must make decisions based on what the individual would have done under the same circumstances, if this can be determined. If this is not possible, then the decision should be based on what is in the individual's best interests. Refer to Chapter 6 for detailed guidance on how to make medical decisions on behalf of someone else.

2

The Guardianship Process

Due Process Protections

States provide specific due process protections for an individual who is the subject of a guardianship proceeding. The most basic protections include the rights to the following:

- Receive notice of the guardianship proceeding
- Be represented by an attorney
- Have a hearing on the need for a guardianship
- Be present at the hearing and all other court proceedings
- Compel witnesses and confront and cross examine all witnesses
- Present evidence
- Have the need for guardianship proven by "clear and convincing" evidence
- Receive notice of all guardianship orders
- Appeal the court's determination

Petitioning

The first step in the legal process of establishing a guardianship is the filing of a **petition**. Proposed guardians, especially family members, may be very involved with the gathering of the information necessary to prepare the petition and preparing for a hearing. The following information may be required to be set out in the petition to determine incapacity:

- Petitioner's name, age, address, and relationship to the person who is subject to the guardianship petition (typically called the **respondent**, or **alleged incapacitated** person)
- Name, age, address, county of residence, and primary spoken language of the respondent
- Names, addresses, and relationships of any known next-of-kin of the respondent
- Specific circumstances that indicate the need to appoint a guardian
- Factual information as to the respondent's incapacity or disability
- Names and addresses of individuals who have knowledge of such factual information

- Rights that the respondent is thought to be incapable of exercising
- Type of guardianship the respondent may need
- A statement that there are no alternatives to address the respondent's problems
- Whether respondent has an agent under a power of attorney or a representative payee for Social Security or other governmental benefits
- Reports of medical or psychological assessments from medical professionals
- Qualifications of the proposed guardian

It is preferable that the proposed guardian not be the petitioner. However, in those circumstances that the petitioner is also the proposed guardian, care must be taken to avoid any **conflict of interest** in bringing the petition. If the proposed guardian is not a family member, it is better practice to have the petition filed only upon referral from a neutral party.

When the proposed guardian is not a family member, he or she should work closely with the attorney for the person facing guardianship when preparing for the court hearing, keeping in mind the following duties:

- Meet the person prior to the hearing
- Determine who has the responsibility to ensure the appearance of the person facing guardianship
- If asked to testify, give direct answers to questions posed by an attorney or judge and respond only with firsthand knowledge

Pre-hearing Process

Before the guardianship hearing takes place, the court most likely will appoint an attorney to represent the individual, if he or she does not have legal counsel. The attorney representing the person who is the subject of the guardianship proceeding should be a zealous advocate for the rights of the person. That attorney should provide any advice using terms the person is most likely to understand.

The court may also direct a **court visitor**, court investigator, examining committee, or **guardian ad litem** to visit the individual and the proposed guardian. The responsibilities of court visitors or other entities involved in the pre-hearing review process vary depending on the state. In general, they assist the court in investigating the circumstances giving rise to the filing of the petition, ways to avoid or limit the guardianship, and the qualifications of the proposed guardian.

Hearing Process

Respondents, or individuals who have had a guardianship petition brought against them, always have a right to attend the hearing. In most states, the court is required to make a finding as to any reason why the person is not able to attend or why attending would be detrimental to his or her well-being. Every effort should be made to explain to the person what will happen at the hearing and ensure that arrangements are made to get the person to the hearing. The court may have the option hold the hearing outside of the courtroom in a place that is convenient to the person facing guardianship, such as the nursing facility or hospital room. The person also has the right to testify if he or she wants to do so. Proposed guardians should attend and may also testify, particularly if it is necessary to establish their qualifications to serve.

The hearing may take minutes or be spread out over weeks, depending on the court and the complexity of the case. The court receives evidence, including any written reports from examining physicians, mental health professionals, guardian ad litem, or court visitors, as well as oral testimony from others who are familiar with the reasons why a guardianship may be necessary and who is best to serve.

The court's determination that an individual is incapacitated and in need of a guardian is a legal, not a medical, finding. This determination should be supported by clear and convincing evidence of a functional impairment which has persisted, or will persist, for a significant period of time. A **functional assessment** by a qualified professional is a significant step in providing the court with the information it needs to make an incapacity determination. This assessment should be done in the person's usual environment with consideration for the individual's privacy and dignity. If the assessment has not been done prior to the filing of the petition, the court may order one to be conducted prior to the hearing.

At the hearing, the court may grant the petition, modify the petition, and grant fewer powers than those requested in the petition, or appoint a guardian other than the party nominated in the petition. The court may dismiss the petition altogether if the evidence given does not prove incapacity.

Once the person has been found to be legally incapacitated and a guardian is appointed, the individual comes under the jurisdiction of the court and is generally known as a person under guardianship. In some states, however, the person may be called a protected person or incapacitated person. It is best practice to use person-first language whenever and wherever possible; therefore, "person subject to guardianship" should be used in place of "incapacitated person." The use of the word "ward" should be avoided, although this term is still used in many state statutes. The person to whom the authority has been delegated to exercise the rights and powers on behalf of the incapacitated person is usually known as the guardian, but he or she may also be called the **conservator** or tutor.

Guardian Qualifications

The qualifications outlined in state statutes for individuals who serve in the powerful position of guardian may be quite minimal, despite the potential for exploitation, neglect, mismanagement, or theft by a guardian. Most state statutes permit any individual over the age of 18 who has not been convicted of a felony to serve as guardian. Also, statutes often authorize a public entity or corporation such as a bank, trust department, or a private or not-for-profit corporation to be appointed as guardian. A few states require that newly appointed guardians complete a specific course or training program on their duties and responsibilities. Some states require a non-family member guardian to be certified by the Center for Guardianship Certification or be licensed by a state agency. Background checks, fingerprinting, or affidavits of fitness may be required in some states.

Surety Bond

A surety bond is sometimes required to protect the person's assets in the event of loss caused by guardians through mismanagement or theft. The bond is like an insurance policy to guarantee that the person will be reimbursed if the guardian does something illegal or unethical with the person's money. The premium will be some percentage of the value of the **estate** and, depending on state law, may be paid out of the person's funds (Standard 18.IV).

The court may waive this surety bond when the person has minimal assets. Regardless of the size of the estate, bonding is often waived for family guardians. It may also be waived for governmental agencies and not-for-profit corporations, if they maintain adequate insurance against all types of loss, theft, or mismanagement.

Authority to Act

The rights that have been removed and delegated to the guardian are stated in an order or judgment signed by the court. In most states, the guardian will get a document called the **letters of office**. This legal document gives the guardian the authority to act on behalf of the person under guardianship and should be recognized by other professionals, banking institutions, government agencies, and service providers. These professionals will want to have certified copies of the judgment, order, or letters of office to verify the areas of authority, such as residential and medical decision making, given to the guardian.

The guardian may exercise only those rights that are listed in the letters of office or **court order** (Ethical Principle 8 and Standard 2.I). In many states, guardians may be prohibited from acting in certain instances without first obtaining approval from the court. Such instances may include sterilization, abortion, forced mental health treatment, experimental medical procedures, residential placement, removal of life support, sale of real and some personal property, payment of guardian or attorney fees, or payment of extraordinary costs. Most of these exclusions represent the most extensive abridgment of an individual's personal autonomy and civil rights (Standard 2.II).

It is essential that guardians be familiar with all state laws, court procedures, and reporting guidelines in their jurisdiction. Because state laws are subject to periodic amendment through legislative action, it is important to stay abreast of any changes that may affect guardianship practice.

Working with the Guardian's Attorney

An important task for the guardian is choosing the right attorney(s). Once this is done, here are eight simple rules to remember:

- The attorney represents the guardian. Guardians have the right and the responsibility to hire and fire their attorney just as they have the right and responsibility to hire and fire any other professional involved in the guardianship (Standard 5.V).
- Use the expertise of the attorney as a guide through difficult and challenging situations.
- Consult the attorney when unsure how to proceed in the guardianship.
- Mistakes happen. Be upfront and honest with the attorney.
- Cultivate the attorney–guardian relationship to the point that each can anticipate the other's needs and methods of handling the guardianship.
- Insist that the chosen attorney timely respond to questions, phone calls, requests for various petitions, etc. This helps the guardian be more effective and timely in administering the guardianship and serving the person under guardianship.
- Work with more than one attorney. The guardian should use the expertise of different attorneys to meet the specific needs of each person under guardianship. In this way, both will learn from and teach the other.
- Make the attorney look good. Just as guardians expect attorneys to be responsive to their needs, attorneys expect the same from guardians.

Notification of Appointment

Many people need to know of the guardian's appointment (Standard 13.V.C). Use this checklist to make sure that all interested parties are notified:

- Family members
- Person's employer, if working
- Any other guardian for the individual
- Agent with a power of attorney (health and financial)
- Health care providers
- Service providers (residential, therapeutic, and day program)
- Government agencies, such as Social Security, from which the person receives payments

- People who owe the person money
- People the person owes money to
- Post office, if the person's mail will be forwarded to a new address
- Anyone involved in a lawsuit by or against the person

The guardian of the estate should also notify:

- Banks, savings and loans, credit unions, and other financial institutions
- Financial advisers
- Insurance companies and agents
- Retirement plans
- County recorders in all counties where the person may own real estate
- Social Security, Veterans Affairs, and Medicaid, as appropriate

Multiple Guardianship Cases

When providing guardianship services to a number of persons, the professional guardian must institute a system to evaluate the needs of each person under guardianship and indicate the complexity of the decisions to be made or the estates to be managed. Guardians must limit the size of their caseloads to a number that allows them to support and protect each person. The size of the caseload must be based on an objective evaluation of the activities expected, time that may be involved in each case, and other demands upon the guardian. The National Guardianship Association (NGA) advocates for monthly guardian visits with each person under guardianship (Standard 13.IV). This minimum standard should be strongly considered in determining the number of persons a guardian can responsibly handle (Standard 23).

Guardianship Service Fees

Guardians are entitled to reasonable compensation for the services provided (Standard 22.I). Fees or expenses the guardian charges must be documented through detailed records of time spent, activities conducted, and expenses incurred to justify any payment from the funds of the person under guardianship (Standard 22.IV). Each person should be charged only for the guardianship services provided to that individual.

All payments from a person's funds to the guardian are subject to applicable laws, court rules, review, and approval (Standard 22.V). In most states, guardians petition the court for an order authorizing collection of reasonable fees and costs from the person's estate. In some cases, the court's original judgment or order may authorize the guardian to collect fees from the estate. In other jurisdictions, a court order must be obtained before paying fees and expenses (Standard 22.III).

The fees must be reasonable, well documented, and related to the guardianship duties. Clear and accurate documentation should include the date and time, service rendered, expenses incurred, and identification of the individual who performed the service, such as the guardian, support staff, or other employee (Standard 22.VIII).

Guardians should realize that the court may consider a number of factors to determine if a fee request is reasonable:

- The powers and responsibilities under the court appointment
- The necessity of the services
- The request for compensation in comparison to a previously disclosed basis for fees, and the amount authorized in the approved budget
- The guardian's expertise, training, education, experience, professional standing, and skill, including whether an appointment in a particular matter precluded other employment
- The character of the work to be done, including difficulty, intricacy, importance, time, skill, or license required, or responsibility undertaken
- The conditions or circumstances of the work, including emergency matters requiring urgent attention, services provided outside of regular business hours, potential danger (e.g., hazardous materials, contaminated real property, or dangerous persons), or other extraordinary conditions
- The work actually performed, including the time actually expended, and the attention and skill level required for each task, including whether a different person could have rendered the service better, cheaper, or faster
- The result, specifically whether the guardian was successful, what benefits to the person were derived from the efforts, and whether probable benefits exceeded costs
- Whether the guardian timely disclosed that a projected cost was likely to exceed the probable benefit, affording the court the opportunity to modify its order in furtherance of the best interest of the estate
- The fees customarily paid, and time customarily expended, for performing like services in the community, including whether the court has previously approved similar fees in another comparable matter
- The degree of financial or professional risk and responsibility assumed
- The fidelity and loyalty displayed by the guardian, including whether the guardian put the best interests of the estate before the economic interest of the guardian to continue the engagement
- The need for a local availability of specialized knowledge and the need for retaining outside fiduciaries to avoid conflict of interest (Standard 22.VII)

Quality Assurance for Guardianship Services

Professional guardians should facilitate a periodic review of their own guardianship services. NGA best practices recommend that an independent review be conducted no less often than every two years. Independent reviews may be obtained from the court monitoring systems, an independent peer, or a Center for Guardianship Certification (CGC) National Master Guardian (NMG) (Standard 24).

Independent reviews involve the following:

- Review of policies and procedures
- Review of a representative sample of case records
- Visits with the clients
- Meetings with clients' care providers

3

Rights of Individuals Under Guardianship

Rights Removed or Delegated

Once the court determines that a person is legally incapacitated, it has the authority to remove certain rights and, if necessary, delegate them to the guardian to exercise on behalf of the person. The rights that are affected by the guardian's appointment vary from state to state. Personal rights that may be removed, but cannot be delegated to another, include the right to:

- Marry
- Vote
- Have a driver's license
- Travel
- Seek or retain employment
- Own or possess firearms or weapons

Rights that may be removed and then delegated to the guardian could include the right to:

- Determine residence
- Consent to medical or mental health treatment
- Manage property and assets
- Contract
- File or defend law suits
- Change marital status
- Apply for government benefits
- Make gifts or dispose of property
- Make decisions about social environment, education, or habitation

Rights Retained

Even though adults under guardianship may lose certain rights during the guardianship process, they retain all other rights. It is the guardian's responsibility to make sure these rights are not violated. These rights include all those guaranteed by federal and state constitutions and laws as well as the specific rights to:

- Be treated with dignity and respect (Ethical Principle 1 and Standard 3.I)
- Be protected against abuse and neglect (Standard 12.I.A)
- Have safe, sanitary, and humane living, working, and learning environments, which are the least restrictive for the person's needs and conditions (Standard 8)
- Have privacy, including the right to bodily privacy and the right to private and uncensored communication with others by mail, telephone, or personal visits (Standard 11)
- Express religious preferences in the manner of his or her choice (Standard 10)
- Have interpersonal relationships and sexual expression (Standard 10)
- Exercise control over all aspects of life that the court has not delegated to the guardian (Standard 9.I)
- Receive appropriate services suited to the person's needs and conditions, including mental health services (Standard 12.I.C)
- Have the guardian advocate for the person's personal desires, preferences, and opinions particularly in regards to ethnic, religious, and cultural values (Ethical Principle 4 and Standard 10.I)
- Exercise the option to procreate (Standard 10.II.C)
- Receive equal treatment under the law, regardless of race, religion, creed, sex, age, marital status, sexual orientation, or political affiliations
- Have explanations for any medical procedures or treatment, including information about the benefits, risks, and side effects of the treatment, and any alternative procedures or medications available (Standard 14)
- Have personal information kept confidential including withholding certain information the person may not want his or her family to know (Standard 11.V)
- Receive prudent financial management of property and information regarding how that property is managed (Standard 17)
- Receive notice of all proceedings related to the guardianship
- Review personal records, including medical, financial, and treatment records
- Speak privately with an attorney or other **advocate**
- Petition the court to modify or terminate the guardianship including the right to meet privately with an attorney or other advocate to assist with this legal procedure
- Have the guardian available to meet the needs of the person at all times
- Receive continuous review of the need for full or partial restoration of rights (Standard 2.VIII)
- Bring a grievance against the guardian or request the court to review the guardian's actions

- Request removal and replacement of the guardian, or request that the court restore rights if it is shown that the person has regained capacity to make some or all decisions (Standard 21.III)

The guardian also has a responsibility to inform the court of any change in the capacity of the person and request that the person's rights be restored when there is evidence that the person has regained capacity (Standard 2.VIII).

4

Roles of the Guardian

Guardian as Surrogate Decision Maker

Guardians have many roles in carrying out their responsibilities. Every guardian needs to be a surrogate decision maker, an advocate, a coordinator of services, a monitor of services, and a financial manager. Guardians must also have some knowledge of law, medicine, psychology, banking, pharmacology, insurance, real estate, accounting, and human nature. They should be compassionate, persistent, a good negotiator, and not easily flustered. In many instances, they need to be prepared to be available "on-call" 24/7.

The fundamental responsibility of the guardian is to make decisions about the person's personal and financial affairs, as ordered by the court. In doing so, guardians should exercise the utmost care and diligence, always with the idea of protecting the self-reliance, autonomy, independence, and rights of the person.

While most guardianship statutes and court orders describe what decisions guardians are authorized to make, most give little guidance on how to make those decisions. The NGA Standards are useful in helping guardians understand the "how-to" of surrogate decision making.

Person-Centered Decision Making and Planning

The person under a guardianship should be at the center of all decisions and plans for the future. We call this being "person centered." Person-centered decision making requires the guardian to identify and advocate for the individual's goals, needs, and preferences. Currently expressed wishes or spoken choices of the person should be supported to greatest extent possible. Goals are what are important to the person, whereas preferences are specific expressions of choice.

NGA Ethical Principle 2 states: A guardian involves the person to the greatest extent possible in all decision making. Whenever possible, the person should be consulted and encouraged to make choices to the extent he or she is able. This includes participating in the decision-making process and acting on his or her own behalf in appropriate instances. The person should be provided with every opportunity to exercise individual rights to the extent he or she is capable. In making a person-centered decision, the guardian shall first ask the person what he or she wants. If the person has difficulty expressing what those wants, the guardian shall do everything possible to help the person to communicate.

Person-centered planning refers to a family of approaches designed to guide change in a person's life. This type of planning is carried out in alliance with the person, their family, and their friends, and is grounded in demonstrating respect for the dignity of all involved. The intent is to discover and understand the unique characteristics of the person so that he or she has positive control over the life desired; is recognized and valued for contributions to the community; and is supported in a web of relationships within his or her community.

Person-centered planning requires the guardian to actively engage the person in the planning process. Let the person identify what is important, what the goals should be, and what makes him or her happy. The root of a strong person-centered plan is separating "important to" from "good for." This moves planning away from an emphasis on health and safety to giving happiness and self-determination more prominent roles. If the person's disability hinders his or her involvement, the guardian will need to research the person's known preferences to augment the planning while continuing to find successful communication avenues (Standard 9).

Substituted Judgment

If a person's incapacity prevents the guardian from effectively determining the person's current wishes in order to make a person-centered decision, the guardian may utilize the principle of **substituted judgment** in making decisions on behalf of the individual.

This principle requires the guardian or other surrogate to learn as much as possible about the lifestyle, behaviors, preferences, and decisions made by the person prior to the incapacity. Taking these factors into careful consideration, the guardian makes decisions that would, as closely as possible, reflect what the person would have decided, if capable of making the decision. The person's autonomy, values, beliefs, and preferences usually are best protected when the person's own judgment can be substituted in place of the guardian's judgment (Standard 7.III).

To do this properly, the guardian must become a detective, carefully unraveling the person's history by consulting anyone who may be able to provide information on the person's preferences and past history of decision making, including the person, the person's relatives, friends, caregivers, or religious leader.

Best Interest

In some instances, the guardian may not be able to determine the person's current wishes or what he or she would have chosen to do on a particular issue. This may occur when the person can no longer communicate his or her wishes or when there is no history of decision making because the person has never had capacity (perhaps due to a severe intellectual disability). In some cases, the guardian may not be successful in locating anyone who has information about the person's previous history.

In these situations, the guardian should make decisions based on the **best interests** of the person. The principle of best interest is based not on the person's history or desires, but on what a "reasonable person" would do. Although the best interest principle is more objective and many factors are weighed in making the decision, it provides the least amount of involvement by the person in the decision-making process. Even when using the best interest standard, the guardian must select the least intrusive, least restrictive, and most normal, course of action (Standard 7.IV).

NGA's position is that the guardian should use the principle of best interest only when person centered decision making or substituted judgment cannot be used. This is when the guardian cannot determine what the person's own decision is or would have been, or when following the person's wishes would cause substantial harm (Standard 7.IV).

When making a decision based on the best interest principle, the guardian should seek expert advice from other professionals or from a special ethics committee. Keep in mind that the determination of what is in the best interest of the individual does not include what the guardian personally thinks would be best for the individual.

Informed Consent

For any person's consent to be valid, it must meet certain legal requirements. To be considered legally adequate, the person giving consent must:

- Be of legal age
- Not have been adjudicated incompetent (as in under a guardianship) or otherwise had the right to consent limited (as in a divorce decree limiting the non-custodial spouse from consenting to services or treatment for a minor child)
- Know and understand the nature, purpose, consequences, risks, benefits, and alternatives to the service or treatment for which consent is being given
- Give the consent voluntarily, without coercion or undue influence from others

If these requirements are met, the individual may give consent. If any of these requirements is not met, an informed consent cannot be made (Standard 6).

A guardian may be called upon to provide informed consent on behalf of the person under guardianship who may be disqualified by one of the above reasons from providing informed consent on his or her own. Guardians providing informed consent on behalf of another are entitled to the same information the person would need to make the consent if he or she were not under guardianship (Standard 6.IV). Refer to Chapter 6 for the steps guardians take in providing informed consent on behalf of a client.

Decision-Making Process

The responsibility of making decisions for another individual on a daily basis both characterizes and sets apart the role of guardian from that of any other service provider. Unlike other professionals, such as physicians, educators, or architects who provide a service at the direction of the client, the guardian provides direction for the client. Just as a professional guardian's role is different than other professionals, a family guardian's role is different than a family member's role. Family members who are appointed as guardian for a loved one need to keep in mind that the decision process is legally different for a court-appointed guardian than for a parent, spouse, sibling, child or other family member who is helping a loved one.

When making any decision on behalf of the person, the guardian should take into consideration the following factors:

- The person should be involved in the decision-making process to the greatest extent possible. The guardian should support the person to make the decision on their own (Standard 9).
- Do everything possible to help the person express his or her goals, needs, and preferences, if the person has difficulty expressing what he or she wants.
- Determine the person's current wishes and desires, if they are ascertainable. Many individuals, regardless of their legal capacity, can express an opinion if approached in a manner they can understand. The guardian should consider the effect the information will have on the person, the person's potential reaction to the information, and what can be done to help the person deal with the information (Standard 9).
- Consider the wishes and desires the person expressed prior to incapacity, if they can be determined. Advance directives, such as a power of attorney or a living will, may provide insight into how the person would have responded to similar situations. The guardian should also ask about clearly communicated oral statements that the person may have made, especially those made to individuals in positions of trust, such as physicians, attorneys, counselors, and faith-based leaders.
- Consider information about how the person would have made the decision. This would include the person's religious, moral, and ethical beliefs. The guardian should also consider any past situations in which the person has made decisions, particularly in which the person has refused medical care.
- Diligently seek the opinions of those familiar with the person, including spouse, parents, children, and next of kin. In evaluating these opinions, it is important to consider any possible distortion in any family member's perception of the situation. Conflicts of interest or lack of involvement with the person may have significant impact on the recommendations that others make.
- Consider the financial consequences to those who express an opinion. Evaluate both the financial advantages and disadvantages to the person's family,

physicians, attorneys, and friends. Also consider the extent to which the consequences of the decision may influence the opinions given.

- Diligently seek the opinions of others who know the person, such as close friends, neighbors, health care workers, etc.
- Consider the opinion of the person's attorney and guardian ad litem, if available.
- Obtain independent opinions from experts and authorities, when necessary.
- Seek opinions from medical or long-term care facility ethics committees or review boards, if available. This may not be possible because not all facilities have an ethics committee or a review board. If they do, they may have a policy against providing an opinion when a conflict of interest exists. In these situations, the guardian should consider presenting the situation to an independent ethics committee, peer review committee, or some other independent review process.
- Document and carefully review any opinions or additional information provided.
- Evaluate the advantages and disadvantages of the decision.
- Modify the person's plan of care in light of the decision that is made. The decision may require that new or additional services be provided.

Only when these steps have been conducted and the goals and preferences cannot be ascertained may the guardian make a decision in the person's best interest (Standard 7.IV).

Least Restrictive Alternative

When supporting the decision of the person or acting as a surrogate decision maker, the guardian must seek the least restrictive alternative or option available that meets the person's needs (Ethical Principal 3). This frequently requires a balance between protecting the person from harm and enhancing the person's self-determination (Standard 8).

In determining the least restrictive alternative for a person, the guardian must:

- Become familiar with available community options for residential placement, medical services, vocational training, and educational services.
- Know the person's goals and preferences, if possible. What the person wants may not be the least restrictive alternative in the guardian's eyes. However, if what the person wants meets the balance between safety and independence and contributes to the person's well-being, then this would be the least restrictive alternative.
- Consider the needs of the person as determined by professionals. This may include assessment of the person's functional ability and health status.
- Choose the option that places the fewest restrictions on the person's rights, freedom, and ability to connect with the environment.

Promoting Growth and Self-Reliance

Guardians should be alert to indications that the person's capabilities have changed. When this occurs, the guardian should assist the person in obtaining complete or partial restoration of any legal rights that were removed. The person has a right to challenge the need for guardianship and may retain an attorney to assist in this endeavor. The guardian has an obligation to assist and guide the person in seeking restoration of rights. In no way should the guardian hinder the person's efforts. Full or partial restoration of rights is a great indicator of the guardian's success in fostering the person's independence and self-reliance (Standard 9). Refer to Chapter 9 for more information about modifying or terminating a guardianship.

Guardian's Relationship with Family and Friends

The guardian's relationship with the person's family members and friends should recognize their contribution to the person's qualify of life. Whether a professional or family member, the guardian should encourage, support, and assist the person in maintaining, establishing, or re-establishing contact with other family members and friends, unless to not do so is necessary to protect the person from substantial harm (Standard 4.I.B). Communication and visitation with the family members the individual wishes to associate with should be encouraged. Some states now require guardians to obtain court permission to limit visitation with family members.

To help foster a continuing relationship, the guardian can communicate regularly with family members and friends and involve them in the person's life and in the decision-making process to the extent that their input benefits the person (Standard 4.V). When disposing of a person's assets, family members and friends should be given the opportunity to obtain items of sentimental value. Court approval may be necessary to transfer these assets (Standard 4.III).

The non-family member guardian must avoid developing a personal relationship with the person's family or friends, unless the relationship existed before the guardian was appointed (Standard 3.II).

Guardian's Relationship with Other Professionals and Services Providers

Professionals, such as attorneys, accountants, financial advisors, real estate agents, service providers, and health care providers, should be engaged, as necessary, to meet the person's needs. The guardian should develop a cooperative working relationship with these professionals and all who provide services to the person (Standard 5). The guardian should establish and maintain regular, substantive communication with any other guardian, agent with powers of attorney, **trustee**, federal fiduciary, representative payee, or other **fiduciary** for the person, if such other fiduciary or surrogate decision makers exist.

Monitoring and Court Supervision

Guardians are under the court's jurisdiction and supervision for the entirety of the guardianship. All guardians must be aware of reporting requirements in their jurisdiction and maintain sufficient documentation of their activities to permit timely filing of all required reports (Standard 2.VI). The guardian's records should document all services provided and detail the steps used in the decision-making process.

Reports to the court become part of the court file and are often public documents; the guardian, therefore, must take care when reporting confidential matters. When necessary, the guardian may petition the court to order sensitive portions of the reports to the court be sealed, to be opened only to those showing good cause to the court (Standard 11.V).

Most states require the guardian of the estate to file an inventory shortly after the guardianship is established (Standard 18.VII). This inventory and any supplemental inventories that are filed become the basis for all later financial reports and court oversight of the estate. The guardian of the estate is required to file an annual accounting, which reflects the current financial status of the estate. The accounting must include detailed reporting of all receipts and all disbursements made from the estate. It should be complete, accurate, and understandable (Standard 18.VIII). In addition, the accounting may reflect changes in the status of specific assets. Refer to Chapter 8 for detailed guidance on record keeping and reporting for guardians of the estate.

Grievance Process

Professional guardians need an established procedure for handling grievances or complaints received from those for whom they serve as guardian or other interested parties. It is important to respond in an open and cooperative manner to any such issues. However, guardians must give careful consideration to the confidentiality of information related to their clients (Standard 11).

Complaints will be handled differently depending on who has made the complaint and their relationship to the person under guardianship. Respond to family members' concerns in a positive manner providing whatever information can be released without breaching confidentiality. If necessary, assist family members to better understand the role and authority of the guardian. Complaints or inquiries received from an official source, such as court investigator, department of aging, or long-term care ombudsman, must be addressed in accordance with their legally defined authority to investigate situations.

5

Fiduciary Principles

All guardians—whether a family member, **volunteer**, public, or corporate guardian—are placed in a fiduciary relationship with the person. This means all guardians have a special obligation of trust and confidence, and the duty to act primarily for their clients' benefit. All guardians are subject to high standards of care and guardianship practice in conducting their responsibilities. Guardians with a higher level of relevant skills are held to the use of those skills (Standard 1.IV).

Once a family member becomes the guardian of a relative, they have a new, and perhaps very different, relationship with that individual. While they still remain a parent, sibling, or spouse, after the court appoints them as a guardian their conduct is governed by the following fundamental principles that apply to all fiduciaries.

Guardians owe undivided loyalty to the person under guardianship. The guardian must avoid having any interest, financial, or otherwise, in any business transactions or activity related to the guardianship. In all dealings on behalf of the person, the guardian's actions and motives must be beyond reproach and are open to scrutiny or challenge by any interested individual or entity (Ethical Principle 7).

Guardians must not cause a breach of trust. The guardian must not perform an act that is contrary to the duty of loyalty or any act that is beyond the scope of the authority granted by the court (Standard 2.I). The guardian, for example, must not select a nursing home for a client because the guardian would receive a commission, bonus, or referral fee from the facility. Likewise, a guardian should not select a bank or investment advisor for a person because of personal discounts or favors for the guardian's staff. Relationships developed during a guardianship should not profit the guardian even after the guardianship ends.

Guardians cannot delegate their authority to act to another individual or agency. Although the guardian cannot turn over the decision-making authority to someone else, this does not preclude employing others to carry out the guardian's directions or decisions.

Guardians have an obligation to keep the person's assets safe. The guardian should keep detailed records of all transactions and be able to account for the person's assets at all times. The guardian of the estate must act immediately after appointment to marshal and secure all estate assets (Standard 17.X).

Guardians have a duty to act on claims. The guardian has a duty to take reasonable steps on claims the person has against others whether they occurred during or prior to the establishment of the guardianship. This may entail filing claims or lawsuits against a former guardian, members of the person's family, or third parties who may have caused a loss to the person's estate (Standard 17.XII).

Guardians have a duty to defend claims. The guardian is under a duty to defend any actions that may result in a loss of guardianship assets, unless it is reasonable not to make such a defense. It may not be in the person's best interest to initiate an action based only on principle when the likelihood of recovery or winning is slight, the expense to the estate is great, and the stress to the person is significant (Standard 17.XII).

Guardians must not commingle assets. The guardian must maintain the person's assets in a separate account and not commingle them with any other guardianship accounts or with his or her own personal accounts (Standard 11). This prohibition against commingling several guardianship accounts does not pertain to bank or trust departments or to corporate or public guardians as long as they have the computer capability to maintain accurate records of each person's account.

Guardians must avoid conflicts of interest. Anyone acting in a fiduciary capacity must take care to avoid conflicts of interest. Conflicts include situations in which an individual may receive financial or material gain or business advantage from a decision made on behalf of another, or from any information gained through these fiduciary responsibilities. Situations which may look like a conflict of interest should be handled in the same manner as those in which an actual conflict of interest exists. Full disclosure of all pertinent information to all interested parties, including the client and the court, may permit the individual to act in situations that are either actual or possible conflicts (Ethical Principle 7 and Standard 20).

Guardians must never enter into a transaction in which they will profit in any way. They must not directly or indirectly buy or sell property from the guardianship to themselves, to their relatives, employees, partners, or other business associates. If there is any doubt over the propriety of any proposed action, the guardian should obtain court approval before taking that action.

It is the guardian's duty to administer the person's estate to solely benefit the person. The estate should not be managed for the benefit of the guardian or anyone personally or professionally related to the guardian. This means the guardian should not be designated as the beneficiary on any life insurance policy, or pension or benefit plan of the person, unless such designation was validly made prior to the establishment of the guardianship. There may be situations, however, where the guardian may choose to designate that life insurance policy proceeds be made payable directly to the person's designated funeral service provider.

Guardians should be independent from all service providers. To ensure that the guardian remains free to challenge inappropriate or poorly delivered services and to advocate vigorously on behalf of the person, the guardian should be independent from all service providers (Standard 16.III.2).

The non-family member guardian, whether an individual or an agency, should be a **freestanding** entity that is completely independent from all other agencies or organizations providing services to any clients. Conflicts of interest can arise when the same agency acts as both guardian and care provider, for example. The decisions the guardian makes may not be the result of free and independent choice when the same agency serves as guardian and provides the client's direct care staff and day habilitation programming (Standard 16.III.B). An exception may be made when a guardian can demonstrate unique circumstances indicating that no other entity is available to act as guardian or to administer the needed **direct services**, provided that such exception is in the best interest of the client. Reasons for the exceptions should be documented and may need court approval.

When a guardian program is a part of a larger organization or governmental entity there must be an **arm's-length relationship** with the larger organization or governmental entity and the program must have independent decision-making ability (Standard 16.III.C).

6

Guardian of the Person

The guardian of the person is responsible for the person's personal needs, such as food and shelter, medical care, transportation, **social services**, and education or rehabilitation. The professional guardian does *not* personally provide each of these services but instead has the responsibility to ensure that the appropriate services are provided (Standard 16.III).

Professional guardians must recognize that each of their clients has their own individual needs and desires. Services for an older person may differ greatly from those that the guardian may arrange for a younger person with an intellectual disability. For example, a young adult with an intellectual disability may need supported employment or a daytime habilitation program, while a person who is older may require stimulating daytime activities but may no longer have the need or ability to be employed. The older client may require services for effective pain management or hospice care to prepare for the end of life—services that may not be needed for a younger person.

The guardian of the person must first gather all pertinent information about the individual to be able to develop a plan of care. A plan of care is begun early in the guardianship but completed after a thorough assessment of the individual's goals, strengths, abilities, problems, and special needs. This plan assists the guardian to establish with the person the short- and long-term goals and the strategies needed to achieve them. Personal assessments, medical information, and personal history must all be obtained and studied before appropriate, informed decision making can occur (Standard 13.II).

Needs Assessments

As soon as the guardianship is established, the guardian must conduct a thorough review and evaluation of the person's status and needs. In addition to the guardian's own evaluation, the guardian should also gather and study any other evaluations by other professionals such as community based agencies, hospital or facility social workers, home health care staff, private care managers, or physicians. A guardianship assessment incorporates any functional assessments, health status, medical treatment, and rehabilitation needs (Standard 13.I).

Functional Assessment

A functional assessment measures the individual's abilities in areas such as behavior, health status, and communication skills. It is indispensable in assisting the guardian to fully understand the person's situation and in providing direction as to how to aid the person to remain as independent as possible.

The assessment should also take into account other aspects of the person's life, such as psychological, social, vocational, cultural, and spiritual concerns. The functional assessment should be done within the person's familiar environment and should identify the following:

- Overall level of functioning of activities of daily living (ADLs) that include feeding, bathing, toileting, dressing, ambulation, and grooming as well as instrumental activities of daily living (IADLs) such as personal banking, medication administration, laundry, housekeeping, shopping, arranging transportation, and coordinating medical care
- Specific behaviors, especially in social and interpersonal relationships, that may interfere with decision making
- Decision-making difficulties caused by the person's environment
- Available resources that may assist the person's ability to make decisions

A functional assessment requires information from reliable sources and is an excellent way to measure and document changes in the person's status over time. Many functional assessment instruments can be used in determining a person's abilities and limitations. The person's specific disability may dictate which of these instruments should be used, as some instruments can only be administered by trained professionals. Others are simpler tools capable of being completed by anyone who is very familiar with the person.

Informed Consent

When the person cannot provide informed consent for himself or herself, the guardian of the person with the appropriate authority may be asked to provide consent on behalf of the person. Refer to Chapter 4 for the requirements to make an informed consent.

Some of the situations that call for the guardian to provide informed consent could include the following:

- Routine medical services, as well as surgery
- Residential placements, such as in nursing homes or institutions
- Nonresidential services including home health care, mental health counseling, physical therapy, occupational therapy, and vocational services
- Release of confidential medical or social records for review by other professionals

- Release of others from liability (such as attendance on field trips, special activities, or use of the person's photograph)

When given the authority to exercise informed consent on behalf of another, the guardian stands in place of that person. At a minimum, the guardian should evaluate each requested decision using the following criteria:

- The person's ability to direct the decision or give consent on his or her own
- Preferences the person states currently or stated prior to the guardian's appointment
- A clear understanding of the nature of the request and what it means
- Condition(s) or circumstances giving rise to the need for consent
- Expected outcomes of this decision
- Benefits of this decision
- Consequences, if any, of waiting
- Consequences if the action is not done
- Available alternatives or options
- Risks involved with each alternative
- Documentation in support of or in opposition to the action
- Need for a second opinion
- Information or input from family members or other professionals

Promote the Person's Well-Being

Guardians have an ongoing responsibility to promote the health and well-being of the person. Therefore, the guardian must stay informed about the person's status and needs in order to make decisions that support, encourage, and assist their abilities and preferences. The guardian should also explore opportunities in all areas of life that are important to the individual, taking into account goals, interests, age, and abilities (Standard 12.I.C).

Before consenting to services, the guardian has the responsibility to investigate the services being recommended and to determine the following:

- Purpose of the service including what it is and why it is being recommended
- Goals and objectives for the person in relation to the service
- Available alternatives
- Projected length of time the service will be needed
- Who is responsible for managing the service
- Who is responsible for directing the service staff
- Whether the provider and its staff are qualified to provide the services
- Who will document the person's progress or performance in relation to the service
- Whether other services are needed in conjunction with the service, such as respite services or transportation

- Whether the service is being provided in the least restrictive manner
- Adequacy of funds for the service's duration
- Cost and method of payment

Communication Skills

Effective communication is an important tool for all guardians. When communicating with clients, the guardian should:

- Talk with, not at, the person
- Listen carefully to what they are saying or trying to communicate
- Include them in the conversation
- Never discuss them as though they are not there
- Encourage them to answer questions directed to them
- Consult with them, even on "minor" issues
- Include them in any meetings affecting their future
- Avoid nicknames and terms ("honey," "gramps," etc.) which have a childish or disrespectful connotation
- Introduce them using their full name and using a title such as Mr., Mrs., or Miss to show respect
- Address them by any preferred name or title

Guardians should model the behavior they expect service providers to follow when communicating with or otherwise relating to the person. The way the guardian interacts with the person, the way the guardian speaks about or to the person, and the way the guardian treats the person can serve as behavioral models for others.

Guardian as Advocate

Advocacy is defined as the act of pleading for, defending, supporting, or espousing a cause. This definition takes on special meaning when the advocacy is associated with persons who are incapacitated and are unable to intercede on their own behalf.

The advocacy role is an integral part of the guardian's responsibilities because the guardian coordinates the person's support, care, comfort, and health (Ethical Principle 4). The guardian also monitors the appropriateness of services and ensures that the person receives all entitlements for which the person is eligible. The following are some of the areas in which a guardian will be advocating on behalf of the person:

- Freedom from abuse and neglect
- Privacy
- Quality of personal care
- Appropriate, least restrictive living arrangements, including in-home care (Standard 12.I.A)

- Employment
- Educational, vocational services, and day habilitation
- Access to community services, including transportation
- Access to public buildings
- Entitlements and benefits
- Basic civil and property rights
- Religious rights
- Medical rights, including mental health services
- Parental rights
- Uncensored communication
- Confidentiality (Ethical Principle 6 and Standard 11)
- Sexual expression (Standard 10)

Guardian's Personal Involvement

The non-family member guardian should develop and maintain a meaningful relationship with the person to gain valuable insight and firsthand knowledge of the person's needs, comforts, satisfactions, and desires. Regular contact with the person promotes trust and confidence and facilitates discussion of difficult issues such as life-support preferences, treatment during serious illness, and burial preferences.

Encouraging the person to relate personal stories and express opinions can also provide information about the person's wishes and lifestyle preferences. It is important to remember, however, that it is not the guardian's role to become a substitute family member. The professional guardian should avoid personal relationships with the family. The guardian must avoid developing a personal or sexual relationship with the person, unless the relationship existed before the guardian was appointed (Standard 3).

Care Plans

The guardian serves as coordinator and monitor of the services provided to the person. As such, the guardian should be in control of the overall plan of medical and personal care for the person. To perform the role of coordinator of services effectively and efficiently, it is essential that the guardian develop and maintain a working knowledge of the services, providers, and facilities available in the community (Standard 13.V).

The guardian must be educated about and be able to develop a person-centered guardianship care plan. See Chapter 4 for additional explanations of person-centered planning. In creating a person-centered plan, a person's circle of support should include everyone that is important to the person and who can assist in supporting the person and the care plan. The guardian must remember that each person has unique problems, needs, and desires. Each person is entitled to have an individualized person-centered plan of care to meet those needs (Standard 13.II). To accomplish this, the guardian must:

- Identify the person's preferences
- Determine the person's current wishes
- Identify not only what will keep the person safe but what will keep the person happy
- Distinguish what is important to the person from what is important for person
- Assess the person's needs and strengths
- Identify the individuals who comprise the person's circle of support
- Identify the appropriate resources and service providers
- Arrange for the provision of services
- Monitor the appropriateness and effectiveness of all services
- Continually monitor the person's progress

Some jurisdictions require that the guardian develop a written plan of care as a baseline for future reports on the person's progress. Whether or not the court requires these reports, a guardian must establish a written care plan that includes goals with time frames and how these goals may be achieved. The guardian may use a number of resources to develop this care plan, including the person's physicians, therapists, providers, caregivers, family members, friends, and any special consultants. Include to the fullest extent the person in the plan's creation.

Residential facilities and day programs also conduct periodic care plan conferences to evaluate the status of the person and any problems that may need attention. The department heads from nursing, dietary, occupational and physical therapy, and social services usually attend these conferences along with the director of activities. The guardian should always attend these conferences to provide input, discuss the person's progress, and provide approval for implementation of the proposed care plan. The person should also attend and be at the center of the discussion (Standard 13.IV.C).

Monitor Medical Status

Information about the person's current and past medical status must be obtained from physicians, psychiatrists, therapists, and other health care providers (Standard 13.I.C). Thoroughly review hospital discharge summaries and facility care-plan records. The newly appointed guardian should immediately obtain a current medication review (including regularly used over-the-counter medications and supplements) from a pharmacist or knowledgeable physician. It is not uncommon to discover that the person has been taking numerous medications for a long period of time without appropriately coordinated medical supervision. As a result, the individual may be confused or disoriented, experience memory loss, or exhibit aggressive or combative behavior. A pharmacological review can clarify whether the medications continue to be appropriate. The guardian should also inquire whether newer medications with fewer side effects may be more effective. Have readily accessible a medication list for each client.

Monitor Care and Treatment

The care and treatment the person receives should be monitored on an ongoing basis to ensure that they conform to the care plan and continue to be appropriate. The guardian should observe and evaluate the results of all treatment services and discuss any changes that may be necessary or advantageous (Standard 13).

The guardian has the right to review the person's medical records at any time, including recent medication changes and social service notes. In particular, medications should be monitored to make sure that no medications are given to make the person easier to manage for the convenience of staff.

To facilitate open communications, establish a working relationship with staff members who are providing services. Guardians should remain in frequent contact with all service providers and regularly inspect any records or notes about the person (Standard 13.IV.B). The person's direct service staff, particularly those seeing the person daily, often have the best and most current information and can more easily detect changes in the person's condition.

Make regular personal visits to monitor the person's progress and to ensure that all necessary services are being provided. Through these visits, the guardian obtains firsthand information about the adequacy of the services being provided. NGA believes that the best standard of guardianship practice requires that these visits be conducted at least monthly (or more often if the person's needs warrant) (Standard 13.IV). The frequency of these visits may be dictated by state law, local rule, or by a guardianship agency's policies.

Use Available Community Resources

The guardian works as the leader of a team to ensure care and services. As the informed decision maker acting with and on behalf of the person, the guardian has the responsibility to ensure the use of quality and cost-effective community resources. Resources available through state, county, or private agencies may include the following:

- Case management
- Transportation
- Home health care
- Home-delivered meals

- Day treatment
- Special recreational programs
- Sheltered or supported employment

It is important to stay abreast of changes in these community resources, as the professional or public guardian is often faced with balancing multiple providers serving a number of persons located in a variety of community settings.

Assist with Finances

When there is no guardian of the estate, the guardian of the person may also have some financial responsibilities (Standard 12.I.G). Those responsibilities, depending on the person's circumstances and the court order, may include the following:

- Assisting with personal budgeting or finances
- Obtaining or maximizing public benefits, such as Social Security or veteran's benefits
- Making pre-need funeral and burial arrangements
- Assisting in estate planning to the extent allowed by state law

Determining Residence

The person's living situation must be evaluated for appropriateness, health and safety concerns, and whether it is the least restrictive alternative (Standard 12.I.A). The guardian must always keep in mind that the least restrictive living environment for one person may not be the least restrictive living environment that meets the needs of another person (Standard 8.III).

The many issues the guardian of the person must consider when evaluating the person's ability to remain in the home include the following:

- Available assets and income
- The person's basic needs
- Level of care and services needed
- Availability of needed services
- Transportation to medical care or therapy
- Socialization
- Maintenance of the residence

NGA strongly supports the right of each person to reside in his or her own home or other community-based setting if he or she so wishes. Not all communities have the services to assist the person to do so, and not all persons can afford the services that are available. A person wishing to remain at home, and with adequate resources to do so, should be moved to a more restrictive setting only to prevent substantial harm (Standard 12.I.A.5).

If it is necessary to move the person from the home to another setting, the guardian should choose the least restrictive alternative living arrangement that meets the person's needs for basic care, safety, socialization, and health preservation. If the only alternative immediately available is not the least restrictive placement, the guardian should advocate for a more desirable placement as soon as possible.

Before moving a person to a more restrictive setting, the guardian must evaluate other medical and health care options and make an independent determination that the move is the least restrictive alternative at the time and fulfills the current desires as well as the needs of the person. The guardian needs to apply person-centered decision making and planning skills in this process. Seek the opinions of medical or health care personnel, as well as those most familiar with the person, as to the person's needs and the type of facility that is most appropriate. The guardian should keep in mind the person's personal tastes, lifestyle, and proximity to friends and family when choosing a residential location (Standard 12.I.A.3). Prior to any move, visit the facility and review reports from licensing agencies and boards.

Caregivers and others familiar to the person can assist with preparing the person for the move and making the transition to another level of care less traumatic. Frequent monitoring during the adjustment period is important. Some courts require prior approval before a move to a more restrictive setting (Standard 12.I.A.4).

Addressing Behavioral Problems

If staff at the person's residence reports that the person has behavioral problems that need to be addressed, the guardian should determine:

- That the problem behavior is clearly identified
- What are the risks associated with behavior
- What has been tried to change the behavior
- What is the proposed intervention process
- Who will implement the intervention
- Whether the staff implementing the intervention are properly trained
- That the intervention will be implemented consistently
- Whether the intervention violates the person's rights in any way
- Whether the intervention violates a court order or federal, state, or local statute or rule
- That any rights restriction is outweighed by the risks associated with the behavior
- What are the expected outcomes
- What are the possible alternative outcomes
- Who will record and collect the data on the effectiveness of the intervention process

- Who will interpret this data
- How the intervention process will be monitored
- When the intervention process will be re-evaluated
- What criteria will determine the success of the intervention

Guardians have the substantial responsibility to oversee any medication regime and need to be knowledgeable about the side effects, purpose, and interactions of all prescription and over-the-counter medications the person may be taking. Be alert to the effects that overmedicating and drug interactions can have on behavior and personality. The guardian may need to take extra steps to ensure that care providers and physicians are aware that the guardian should be involved in any discussion about medication change and provide informed consent to any change. The inappropriate use of chemical restraints to control behavior for the convenience of a nursing facility is against the law and is inappropriate in any situation.

Physical Restraints

Physical restraint devices are defined by federal law as "any manual method or physical or mechanical device, material or equipment attached or adjacent to the resident's body that the individual cannot move easily, which restricts freedom of movement or normal access to one's body." This includes belts, vests, pelvic ties, specialized chairs, and bedside rails. A physician's order is required before any restraint can be utilized.

Physical restraints must be used only to treat specific medical or behavioral symptoms and should be tried only after all other methods to improve safety have been exhausted. An individualized care plan should be in place prior to starting the use of a physical restraint. The plan must include monitoring at frequent short intervals for any adverse effect while the restraint is in use. It is essential to remember that commonplace, low-tech devices can be responsible for injury or death through strangulation or entrapment, can increase behavioral problems and physical debility, and can lead to pressure sores and incontinence.

A physical restraint may be necessary for some individuals to provide for their safety. This could include the following:

- Bed rail for someone who is known to fall out of bed while sleeping or who is unable to safely get out of bed, but continues to try to do so
- Wheelchair-positioning belt for an individual who is unable to safely stay seated in the wheelchair
- Helmet for those with frequent uncontrolled seizures
- Gait belt to assist in walking without falling
- Safety vest that prevents an individual from unfastening a seatbelt and moving about in a moving vehicle

Making Medical Treatment Decisions

Medical decision-making for another person is never a simple task. The well-being and comfort of the person—and in some cases, his or her life—depend on the guardian's medical decisions (Standard 14).

Guardians often agonize over how to make the right medical decision, especially when there are several options. Bronchitis, for example, can be treated with as many as 30 different medications, each with its own advantages and disadvantages. When overwhelmed with all this information, the guardian might be inclined to accept the first option presented. This "you're the doctor approach" may not be best for the person under guardianship. Most guardians do not have comprehensive medical and pharmaceutical knowledge, but it is incumbent on them to learn as much as they can about medical conditions and medicines.

Many times, guardians are called upon to make medical decisions under pressure. The diagnosis and recommended course of treatment are given with an expectation that the decisions will be made immediately and simultaneously. It is important for the guardian to know that, although immediate medical decision making might be efficient for the medical provider, it is rarely justifiable on medical grounds. It is very rare that an illness requires immediate action.

In most instances, it is safe to postpone the decision for a few days or until the guardian can obtain enough information to make an informed decision. When a doctor or facility insists on an immediate decision, the guardian should ask if the person's life would be in jeopardy if the decision is postponed for a few days, during which time the guardian can better understand the issues.

Doctors may use vague or technical language when explaining the risks and benefits associated with treatment options. Insist on clarity. For example, if the doctor states that "complications are rare" or "there are seldom any side effects," the guardian should request that these statements be more specifically explained in terms that the guardian can understand.

If the doctor uses words that the guardian does not understand, it is the guardian's responsibility to request clarification. This not only includes non-layman's medical terms but also commonly used words. For example, "successful" may mean various things in medical context. Ask what "successful" means to the doctor. Does it mean that the person will be able to run and hike after knee surgery? Or does it mean simply that the person will have less knee pain?

The medical decision-making process includes many steps (Standard 14). When making medical decisions, keep in mind whether the decision takes into consideration the current wishes of the person, as well as the principles of informed consent, substituted judgment, and best interest. Review Chapter 4 on these topics.

Always consult the person to determine current wishes, keeping in mind the person's:

- Ability to process information
- Mental state

- Emotional state, which can be affected by medications or ineffective pain management
- Potential of being influenced by others

Also consider the psychological effect when receiving information about an untreatable or terminal condition. In those cases, it may be necessary to provide additional support, hospice services, or counseling. The guardian needs to, whenever possible, provide all pertinent information to the person unless the guardian is reasonably certain that substantial harm will result from providing such information.

Consider the person's wishes and desires expressed prior to incapacity. Obtained copies of any advance directives prepared prior to the guardianship to help determine the person's special instructions or treatment preferences (Standard 14.VI). Consider the person's medical history to determine previous decision-making patterns or positions taken by the person, such as prior refusal for surgery or noncompliance with treatments, procedures, medications, or therapies.

Consult the person's family members, friends, neighbors, and clergy to determine what values of religious beliefs are important to the person, if the person's preferences are unknown or cannot be determined (Standard 14.VII). The guardian should consult the person's family and caregivers to determine what they believe the person wants, keeping in mind whether the decision might present a conflict of interest to the family or caregivers. For example, the family of an older person may not wish to see the person's estate spent on medical procedures they believe will dissipate assets that could be inherited by the family. When the wishes of the person cannot be determined, the best interests of the person, rather than the best interests of the family, should control the decision-making process (Standard 4).

Consult the person's physician to determine available options, the prognosis with or without treatment, and the side effects treatment may have on the person (Standard 14.XIII). Discuss any advance directives and the limitations they may place on treatment options. Some of the issues to address with the physician include the following:

- The degree, duration, and constancy of any pain the person may experience, with and without the proposed treatment
- The person's overall prognosis, with and without the proposed treatment
- The possible side effects or unintended consequences of the treatment
- The likelihood that the person will return to the previous level of functioning

The guardian might request that the discussion of these issues be written into the physician's progress notes in the medical chart.

Obtain a second medical opinion. The second opinion should be obtained from an independent physician who has no ties to the first physician or to the medical facility in which the person is currently receiving care (Standard 14.XI). The second physician should be asked to respond to the same issues addressed by the first physician. Also obtain the opinions of the person's nurses and other direct care staff.

These individuals may have valuable insight into the person's outlook and condition and the prospects with or without the proposed treatment. Evaluate the burdens and benefits of continued treatment.

It may be appropriate to incorporate **palliative care** for persons with serious illnesses when it is an accord with the person's wishes (Standard 14.XV). Palliative care is specialized care that treats the discomfort, symptoms, and stress of that illness. The focus is to provide relief from such symptoms as pain, shortness of breath, fatigue, constipation, nausea, loss of appetite, and problems with sleep. It may also help with the side effects of some medical treatments.

Seek opinions from medical facility ethics committees or review boards. Where **extraordinary medical measures** are being considered, the guardian should seek review by an ethics committee. If available, seek opinions from independent ethics committees with no ties to the facility providing care to the person.

Informal reports to the person's family and friends may help facilitate communication and cooperation that will benefit the person. Keep individuals important to the person reasonably informed about important health care decisions (Standard 14.XVI). The guardian, however, must maintain the confidentiality of the person's affairs (Ethical Principle 6 and Standard 5).

Invasive Medical Procedures

By law in almost every state, guardians do not have the authority to consent to certain invasive medical procedures such as abortion, sterilization, amputation, treatments that may cause permanent damage or disfigurement, **psychotropic medications**, electroshock therapy, drug trials, or experimental medical procedures. Some case law has considered whether a guardian can consent on behalf of the person to bone marrow transplants to aid a family member with leukemia. It is always advisable to consult legal counsel in these instances. The guardian will need to get specific court direction and approval before considering potentially controversial procedures (Standard 14.XIV).

Withholding and Withdrawing Medical Treatment

Always presume to continue medical treatment. However, there are circumstances in which consent to withhold or withdraw medical treatment is legally and ethically justifiable. In these situations, the guardian should follow the wishes of the person as currently expressed or previously stated in an advance directive. Any inconsistency in the person's wishes should be presented to an ethics committee. It may be necessary to ask the court for direction. The guardian should follow the principles of informed consent when making this decision on behalf of the person (Standard 15).

Do Not Resuscitate Orders

Unlike the health care power of attorney a patient fills out, a do not resuscitate (DNR) order is a medical order made by a doctor that is placed in the patient's medical record. The DNR order directs the hospital medical team to not attempt to revive the patient in the event the patient stops breathing or the heart stops beating. The order is entered only in those special circumstances where the doctor has confirmed with the patient, when possible, or the guardian or health care agent that not trying to restore breathing or heart rhythm is the preferred alternative.

Good medical practice and the policies of most health care and residential facilities require that cardiopulmonary resuscitation (CPR) be started in the event the person suffers a heart attack or arrested breathing, unless there is an order to the contrary in the patient's chart. Consent from the patient or the guardian is required for entry of a DNR order. It is not an advance directive.

A DNR order may be an appropriate order for an individual who is critically or terminally ill. An individual who is physically healthy but disabled should not have a DNR order.

Most health care facilities have internal policies specifying such things as:

- Who may give consent for the DNR order
- How long the DNR order is effective
- Whether the facility will recognize a DNR order
- What specific procedures are included in the order

All but six states also have **POLST** (Physician Orders for Life-Sustaining Treatment) protocols. Typically, a state-prescribed POLST form is prepared for very sick patients with multiple chronic conditions. While the details vary from state to state, as well as the name (MOST or POST, for example), in general this protocol is an effort to encourage conversations among medical providers and patients (as well as their guardian and family members) to understand and record the patient's current treatment preferences. It must be signed by the patient or the guardian, as well as the physician. A POLST complements, rather than replaces, an advance directive. It records in detail the decisions the patient makes and puts those decisions into medical orders to be followed in a medical crisis. The form is printed on brightly colored paper so it can be readily seen, followed, and transferred with the patient from hospital to nursing facility and back to the hospital. To find out more about POLST, go to www.polst.org.

Final Arrangements

If the person did not make final funeral and burial arrangements prior to the guardianship, the guardian should attempt to determine the person's preferences about final disposition of the body, funeral services, and burial arrangements. This may be accomplished by consulting the person and the person's family, friends, or religious leader. If the guardian is unable to determine the person's wishes, the guardian should arrange for traditional burial; however, state law, agency policy, and the person's financial status will have an impact on this decision.

When the person has sufficient funds or assets that need to be spent down to qualify for benefits, it is usually a best practice to purchase a prepaid burial plan. Funds set aside to cover these expenses are usually not counted as assets and therefore do not make the person ineligible for Medicaid. There are, however, Medicaid restrictions regarding the amount, portability, and revocability of such burial plans. Consult with legal counsel familiar with your state's Medicaid requirements.

The responsibility and authority to make these arrangements may rest with another fiduciary. If a guardian of the estate or other surrogate decision maker is serving the person, making funeral and burial arrangements should be coordinated with that fiduciary. The guardian of the person should be cautious about taking any action that exceeds the guardian's scope of authority.

7 Abuse and Neglect

A primary responsibility of a guardian is to protect the person from harm. Because of this obligation, the guardian must be alert to all possible forms of abuse, know the local laws that protect people from abuse and neglect, and be aware of the reporting requirements (Standard 12.I.I and Standard 17.XVII).

The basic categories of inappropriate and harmful treatment of vulnerable individuals are as follows:

- *Abuse.* Abuse is usually defined as inflicting physical pain or injury, mental injury, or physiological injury.
- *Neglect.* An example of neglect by someone else is when a caregiver or spouse deprives the person of those services necessary to maintain their health and welfare. A person can also be a victim of self-neglect. Self-neglect occurs when an adult cannot perform or obtain services necessary to maintain their own health or welfare.
- *Exploitation.* Exploitation is the improper use of the adult's resources by a caregiver or someone else for profit or to advantage of the caregiver or others.

State statutes explicitly define these categories of abuse of vulnerable adults. It is imperative that the guardian be familiar with these laws. Depending on state laws, a guardian may be required to report suspected abuse or neglect to the appropriate agency or authority.

Recognizing Neglect and Abuse

One indicator does not necessarily constitute evidence of elder abuse or neglect. Yet, when several indicators are present along with possible injuries, the guardian must further investigate. Whenever a guardian becomes aware of any of the following circumstances, the guardian must consider that some sort of inappropriate care may be taking place.

Physical Abuse

Physical force resulting in bodily injury, physical pain, or physical impairment is the typical definition of physical abuse. This may include striking, hitting, beating, pushing, shoving, shaking, slapping, kicking, pinching, and burning. It also may include the inappropriate use of drugs and physical restraints, force-feeding, and physical punishment of any kind.

Some indicators of possible physical abuse include:

- Self-reports of abuse or rough treatment, such as being hit, slapped, or otherwise mistreated
- Broken bones, skull fractures, sprains, dislocations, internal injuries, open wounds, cuts, and other untreated injuries in various stages
- Bruises in unusual locations that are not consistent with a fall or bumping into furniture
- Open sores or injuries that should be bandaged
- Limbs in awkward positions, which may indicate neglected fractures
- Broken eyeglasses/frames
- Unexplained weight loss or hair loss
- New onset of confusion or disorientation
- Injury not properly cared for
- Pain on touching
- Burns and/or abrasions that may be caused by cigarettes, rope friction, chains, or other means of confinement
- Signs of confinement, such as door locks, restraints, or blocked exits
- Dehydration or malnourishment without illness or other cause
- Pallor, sunken eyes or cheeks
- Bed sores
- Medication administration errors (either too much or not enough)
- Poor skin hygiene, missing hair, or bruising in scalp
- Dirty clothes, bed clothes, or general environment
- Frequent trips to emergency rooms
- Frequent health care shopping among providers
- Lack of necessary walkers, canes, commodes, telephones, teeth, artificial limbs, glasses, or wheelchair
- Lack of heat, food, or water

The guardian may observe behaviors that also raise the question of possible physical abuse, such as:

- Evidence that the person is easily frightened, agitated, or trembling
- Denial of a problem in the face of other possible evidence
- Hesitation to speak openly
- Implausible explanations for injuries
- Depression

Sexual Abuse

Nonconsensual sexual contact of any kind is the broad definition of sexual abuse. Usually, sexual contact with anyone incapable of giving consent is also considered sexual abuse. Sexual abuse can include unwanted touching and all types of sexual assault or battery, such as rape, sodomy, coerced nudity, and sexually explicit photography. However, it is imperative that a guardian fully understand the state's legal definition of sexual abuse. These legal definitions can differ and are often quite explicit.

Some common indicators of sexual abuse include the following:

- Report of being sexually assaulted, abused, or raped
- Extreme agitation when bathed, changed, or examined
- Bruising in the genital or breast area
- Unexplained vaginal or anal bleeding
- Torn, stained, or dirty underclothing
- Genital or urinary irritation, injury, infection, or scarring
- Nightmares, night terrors, or other sleep disturbances
- Phobic behavior
- Extreme anxiety, including difficulty sleeping, eating, fearfulness, or compulsive behavior
- Inappropriate, unusual, or aggressive sexual behavior

Emotional Abuse

Verbal, emotional, or psychological abuse is the infliction of pain or distress through verbal or nonverbal acts. This type of abuse includes verbal assaults, insults, threats, intimidation, humiliation, and harassment. It also includes treating adults like infants; isolation from family, friends, or other regular activities; or care that is depersonalizing or that treats the person as an object.

There may be no physical evidence of this type of abuse, but it is highly correlated to the other types of adult abuse. A guardian suspecting physical or sexual abuse should look for emotional abuse as well.

Indications of verbal, emotional, or psychological abuse may include the following:

- Reports of being verbally mistreated
- Emotional agitation with no apparent cause
- Isolation
- Withdrawn and noncommunicative behavior
- Expressions of a death wish
- Observation of anyone treating the person as a child, using shame or ridicule, or treating the person with contempt
- Isolation from family or friends
- Unexplained weight loss
- Sleep, eating, or speech disorders
- Depression
- Attention-seeking behavior

Caregiver Neglect

Neglect means the refusal or failure to fulfill a person's obligations, duties, or contracted service to a vulnerable adult. This could include the deliberate refusal or failure to provide life necessities such as food, water, clothing, shelter, personal hygiene, medicine, comfort, personal safety, and assistance with activities of daily living. The guardian of person is often responsible for these very areas of care and many times contracts for this care with another provider. It is essential that the guardian understand that caregiver neglect may be indicated by patterns of behavior or through negative or adverse impacts on the person's health and welfare.

Indicators of caregiver neglect may include the following:

- Self-report of being neglected
- Dehydration, malnutrition, untreated bedsores, or poor personal hygiene
- Unattended or untreated physical or mental health problems
- Unsafe living conditions, such as absence of utilities, heat, or running water
- Unsanitary or unclean living conditions, indicated by dirt, fleas, lice, soiled bed linens, fecal or urine smell
- Inappropriate or inadequate clothing
- Being locked in or out of residence
- Inadequate supervision
- Improper administration of medication
- Missed health care appointments
- Failure to follow medical, therapy, or safety recommendations

Improper Residential Care

Any type of abuse may happen when a person is in any type of group setting or institution. It can also happen when a person is living at home receiving care from family members, friends, volunteers, and informal or formal caregivers.

Assuring that a high quality of care is provided is an essential responsibility of the guardian. The following are common indicators for identifying poor care, neglect, or abuse in residential facilities:

- Unanswered call bells or signal lights
- Inappropriate use of physical or chemical restraints
- Excessive use of restraint
- Overuse of sedation
- Infrequent or irregular toileting
- Frequent urinary tract infections
- Diaper use when need is questionable
- Urine and other body odors
- Poor mouth care as evidenced by odors and crusting
- Unshaven facial hair

- Uncombed hair
- Long and dirty fingernails/toenails
- Eyeglasses or dentures locked away or missing
- Skin breakdown on buttocks or in skin folds
- Not offering water to residents, dehydration, excessive thirst
- Dry mouth, eyes sunken, very dry skin, speech problems
- Inadequate assistance with feeding leading to poor nutrition
- Unappealing food, not enough variety, or not enough fluids
- Threats, rough handling, or scolding
- No access to a telephone or no options for privacy
- Refusing to facilitate ombudsman intervention
- Poor staff training
- Inadequate supervision of staff
- Inadequate staffing ratios for number of residents

How the person acts may give further clues that something is not right. Some example of behaviors that may be clues to the occurrence of abuse or neglect include the following:

- Fear, either general or of a specific caregiver
- Being withdrawn
- Depression or sadness
- Feelings of helplessness
- Resignation
- Unwilling or hesitant to speak openly
- Stories which are difficult to believe
- Confusion or disorientation
- Contradictory statements in the absence of mental dysfunction
- Anger
- Unresponsiveness
- Nervousness, anxiety, or agitation

The guardian might pick up other clues and indicators from the care provider's behavior, such as the following:

- Not allowing the person to speak for himself or herself or see others without the provider's presence
- Attitude of indifference, anger, or unwillingness to help
- Blaming the person for being incontinent or forgetful
- Threats, insults, harassment, or other aggressive behavior
- History of abusing other dependent people
- Alcohol or drug involvement
- Flirtatious or coy behavior, which may indicate inappropriate sexual behavior
- Isolating the person from activities, family members, friends, etc.
- Conflicting accounts of incidents

- Unwillingness to comply with care plan implementation
- Unwillingness to cooperate with other providers

If a guardian observes any of these signs of possible abuse or that the person is not receiving proper care, the guardian should further investigate what is happening and take appropriate steps to correct the situation or report to appropriate authorities. If the abuse is happening in a care facility, the long-term care ombudsman should be contacted. Adult protective services laws may require the guardian to report suspected abuse. A physician or other qualified health practitioner must do a physical assessment to conclusively establish physical abuse.

Exploitation

All guardians have the fiduciary responsibility to be aware of any mismanagement or misuse of the person's funds. Monitoring for exploitation and reporting as necessary is essential.

Exploitation is usually defined as the improper or illegal use of a person or a person's funds, resources, or assets. Some examples of exploitation are using the person as an unpaid laborer, cashing checks without authorization or permission, forging signatures, stealing possessions or money, coercing or deceiving someone into signing a document (contract, deed, will, or power of attorney), or improperly using the authority of a guardianship or power of attorney.

Indicators of possible exploitation include the following:

- Self-reports of being exploited
- Social isolation, with few supports or contacts
- Missing property or belongings
- Disappearance of funds or valuable property
- Suspicious signatures on checks or other documents
- Forged signature transferring property or title
- Sudden changes in bank accounts, such as large or unexplained withdrawals
- Addition of names to bank accounts
- Unauthorized use of credit cards or ATM cards
- Abrupt changes in estate-planning documents, deeds, or other financial documents
- Sudden transfer of assets or gifts
- Bills unpaid even when resources are available
- Failure to spend funds on needed services
- Providing services that are unnecessary

Promptly report to appropriate authorities concerns about possible exploitation (Standard 17.XVII).

8 Guardian of the Estate

The court entrusts guardians of the estate with the responsibility to protect and preserve the person's assets and manage the person's affairs with prudence, intelligence, and discretion (Ethical Principle 9). The protection of the person's estate or property from waste, mismanagement, and exploitation is a primary reason that courts appoint guardians of the estate.

The legal responsibilities and duties of the guardian of the property are usually delineated in each state statute and include:

- Who must post a **surety bond**
- When an inventory of property must be filed
- How often accountings are to be filed with the court for review
- What actions are allowed or prohibited
- When the guardian must obtain court approval to act

The day-to-day duties of the guardian of the estate, however, are not usually specifically addressed under state law. While these duties are primarily shaped by the needs of the individual, they may also be influenced by local practice or agency policies. The NGA Standards of Practice provide additional guidance on how to make financial decisions.

While guardianships encompass a wide variety of client groups—from those who have substantial estates to others who have minimal assets—the basic tenets for making decisions about the estate are the same. It is incumbent upon the guardian to apply the fundamental principles of person-centered decision making when state law is silent or vague on specific actions or responsibilities.

Despite the particular circumstances of any guardianship, all decisions involving the estate are governed by the rule that the person's estate is to be used for the benefit of the person, and spouse and/or minor children, if required by state law or court order (Ethical Principle 10 and Standard 17.IX).

Communicating with the Person

The guardian must involve the person under guardianship in estate management decisions to the maximum extent possible. The guardian needs to manage all financial affairs in a way that maximizes the dignity, autonomy, and self-determination of the person (Ethical Principle 1 and Standard 17.I). Guardians must be knowledgeable about the nature of any incapacity or condition of the person so they can better understand his or her abilities, needs, and preferences (Standard 18.II).

Consider the person's wishes, currently expressed or contained in any directives, such as a will, trust, or financial power of attorney (Standard 18.III). The guardian should obtain a copy of the person's will and/or any other estate-planning documents, if any exist (Standard 17.XV). The intentions expressed in these documents are important in determining how to handle estate assets. Exercise caution, however, when considering the person's history of spending or gift giving, as these activities may have been the result of coercion or manipulation. In making financial decisions, give priority to the goals, needs, and preferences of the person while weighing the costs and benefits of each decision to the estate. Utilize the principles of substituted judgment when the person is unable to direct his or her own decisions (Standard 17.II).

Marshal the Estate

Guardians of property must carefully review the court order to determine the powers that have been granted so they can take appropriate action (Standard 2). Consistent with that order, exercise only the authority granted and required to provide for the person (Standard 17.VI). Locate and take control of the person's assets as quickly as possible after appointment (Standard 18.I). A review of the mail will help identify bank accounts, investments, and other assets. Notify the postal service to forward the person's mail to the guardian.

Make an initial search, with a witness, of the residence and change the locks to prevent others from gaining access. If the residence is vacant, notify local police to be alert for intruders or vandals. Take possession of all property to protect it from damage, loss, or destruction, including but not limited to the following:

- Cash
- Wages (some states require an additional court order to control wages)
- Uncashed checks and refunds
- Bank accounts (checking, savings, certificates of deposit)
- Stocks, bonds, mutual funds, brokerage accounts
- Promissory notes, partnerships, other business interests
- Life insurance policies
- Real estate
- Furniture
- Antiques
- Artwork
- Jewelry
- Pets
- Valuable collections (stamps, coins, dolls, etc.)
- Vehicles, boats, trailers

Secure easily transported valuable items by placing them in a safe or locked storage. Determine the durability of stored property as the condition and value of some items may decline over time. Consider storage costs versus value, taking into account the person's sentimental attachment to the belongings.

If the person's residence is an apartment and the person will not return there to live, notify the landlord of the intent to vacate, allowing enough time to remove personal property and to clean the apartment.

If the person owns a residence but is not be living there, check the residence at least once per month and winterize it if necessary. Verify the existence of adequate, paid homeowner's insurance. If the residence remains unoccupied, usually for longer than six months, some insurance companies will not continue to insure the property. A special vacant-property policy should be obtained, if possible. Insurance companies and agents who specialize in providing liability insurance to guardians, especially errors and omissions policies, are sometimes the best resources to consult regarding a vacant-property policy.

Make arrangements to protect the property from waste, dissipation, and deterioration. When necessary, arrange for a company to assist with clean up and monitoring.

Determine whether the property should be leased or whether family members or other interested parties are interested in renting the property and are able to maintain it. If renting the property is being considered, work with an attorney or rental agency to assure that proper procedures are in place to protect and maintain the property. Assess whether there are any environmental issues, such as biohazards and toxic chemicals or waste. It may be necessary to have toxic wastes, such as old paint or herbicides, taken to a proper recycling or disposal center. It may also be necessary to hire a company to deal with larger environmental issues, such as propane gas or oil tanks on the property.

Verify that all property in addition to the dwelling is insured. Check to see if personal property is covered by homeowner's insurance. If not, additional insurance may need to be purchased. Automobiles must be insured even if they are not being driven (Standard 19.V).

Make an inventory of all assets for the court (Standard 18.VII). Depending on the court, it may not be necessary to include in the inventory a detailed list of personal property. In any event, create a detailed listing. This step protects the guardian from family members or others interested parties who may question the existence of certain items. Have at least one other witness sign the inventory and thoroughly photograph or videotape the belongings. A professional, third-party service may be hired to do the inventory, but the guardian should remain present for the entire inventory process. Jewelry, firearms, coins, antiques, or other collectibles should be taken to an appropriate appraiser, or the appraiser may be hired to view the items on site.

Inventory the person's safe deposit box in the presence of a neutral third party or bank official. Create a list of the contents and have all those present sign the inventory.

Open a separate checking account for the person. The account should be a "guardianship" account for the benefit of the person, using the person's Social Security number. After the inventory is complete, transfer current bank balances into the new guardianship account, leaving a sufficient amount in the old account until all checks have cleared and direct deposits or automatic payments have been redirected (Standard 17.X.I).

Obtain legal advice before closing any account or transferring any funds from any account that the person owns jointly with anyone else. These accounts could include checking or savings accounts that are "joint with the right of survivorship" (JTROS), "pay on death" (POD), or "transfer on death" (TOD). In all likelihood, the guardian will need to preserve the same vesting or titling of these accounts.

Determine if there is a cause for legal action to recover or protect assets and contest any questionable claims against the estate. (Standard 17.XII).

Collect all of the income and other money due the person. Apply to be appointed representative payee if the person is receiving Social Security benefits or **federal fiduciary** if the person receives veteran's benefits. A state guardianship order is not sufficient to authorize control over these federal benefits. Notify all other sources of income, including pensions and retirement plans, of the guardianship and direct that all funds be sent in care of the guardian of the estate. It may or may not be possible to control wages depending upon state law.

Maintain the Estate

Work with the person and any guardian of the person to develop a financial plan and budget. The plan should correspond to the person's care plan and focus on his or her goals, needs, and preferences. This plan includes regular monthly expenses such as rent, home care, groceries, or long-term care as well as personal spending money. An additional court order may be required to pay out-of-the-ordinary expenses. Pay the person's bills on time and according to the budget developed. If possible, develop a financial plan for the future needs of the person (Standard 18.III).

Allow the person to manage personal funds to the extent that he or she is able. Some may be encouraged to pay for extras such as cable television out of their spending money while the guardian ensures that housing and food costs are paid.

Interact with the person's spouse and minor children and provide for their needs, as required. Although it may be difficult, try to determine an equitable way to divide financial responsibilities if the person is sharing a household with a spouse. Remember that monetary gifts other than small amounts for birthdays and holidays usually may not be given to anyone without a court order.

Guardians have the duty to apply for all benefits the person may be entitled to receive. Benefits may include Social Security disability or survivor benefits, Medicaid, housing assistance, or low-income loans for home repairs (Standard 18.V).

Keep all property safe and in good repair. Assessing the person's abilities to remain in the home is important. Be aware of the need for stair rails and grab bars. Have an expert look over the property to catch needed repairs early. Check with local nonprofits, such as the United Way, to see if funds are available to help pay for needed repairs. Additionally, the guardian must consult state statues to determine if a court order is needed for necessary repairs.

Retain services of any professionals as needed. Guardians who have little experience in handling complicated estates or specific types of assets, such as investments and pension plans, have the affirmative duty to seek professional assistance. Brokerage accounts or agency accounts through the trust department of a bank are examples of ways to get assistance in handling larger estates. Hiring a professional accountant to prepare income tax returns may also be warranted, especially if the person has a complicated estate or has not filed a recent return. State and federal tax returns must be filed unless the person meets certain criteria. Consult your tax preparation expert to determine who must file.

It may be necessary to liquidate assets to meet the person's needs. Many clients, particularly those in long-term care, regularly spend more than their income each month. In considering whether to dispose of the person's property, be sure to consider whether so doing will benefit the person and whether there is any likelihood that the person will need that property in the future. Take into account the person's current wishes about the property and any provisions in an estate plan. Other considerations include tax consequences, impact on public benefits, and the costs of maintaining the property (Standard 19.III). Remember to petition the court for authority to sell real or personal property, as required (Standard 19.I).

If additional assets are found after the initial inventory is filed with the court, file a supplementary or amended inventory. If the discovery occurs close to the due date of the first annual accounting, include those assets on the accounting.

Maintain accurate and through records of all income and disbursements. Account to the court within the time set by statue or the court for all money coming into the estate, all expenses paid, and all remaining resources in the estate. The accounting must reflect all financial activity that has taken place during the year (Standard 18.VI).

Prudent Investment

To the extent specified in the guardianship order, the guardian's primary duty is to provide for the management and investment of the estate. The guardian should exercise intelligence, prudence, diligence, and avoid any self-interest when managing a person's finances. The guardian should act in a manner above reproach and act only for the benefit of the person.

When investing estate assets, the fiduciary must apply state law regarding prudent investment practices. In most states, guardians are required to invest applying the principles of the **prudent investor rule** (Standard 17.XIII). The prudent investor rule requires that all investments be considered as part of an overall portfolio rather than individually. No investment is inherently imprudent or prudent. The rule recognizes that certain nontraditional investment vehicles may actually be prudent. Under most circumstances, the person's assets must be diversified. The guardian is obligated to spread portfolio investments across asset classes and potentially across global markets to both enhance performance and reduce risk. The possible effects of inflation must also be considered as part of the investment strategy.

Any guardians who are not specifically experienced in fiduciary investment principals must get advice from professional financial advisors who have the appropriate expertise. Fiduciaries who do not use risk reducing strategies may be personally penalized (Standard 17.XIII). A few states have lists of appropriate investments. Be certain to understand all state requirements.

Powers the Guardian May or May Not Have

Every guardian of the estate must be careful not to exceed the authority granted by the court or state law. Guardianship orders or letters of office may specifically delineate and delegate powers. In most states, the law gives very specific instructions as how guardians are to manage a person's property. The guardian needs to be familiar with actions that do and do not require prior court approval. As always, the guardian should consult an attorney and refer to state laws for specific delineation of powers that require court approval (Standard 2.I).

Generally, prior court approval is not required to do the following:

- Retain possession of assets
- Receive assets from other sources such as other fiduciaries or trustees
- Insure assets against damage, loss, or liability
- Pay taxes and assessments on real and personal property including the residence, cars, and boats
- Pay valid encumbrances, such as mortgages or loans
- Pay reasonable living expenses
- Deposit cash assets to the guardianship account
- Apply for benefits on behalf of the person
- Purchase pre-need funeral and burial arrangements

State laws probably require a guardian to obtain court approval for most of the following legal actions. The guardian must always check with an attorney before undertaking any of these:

- Enter into leases
- Abandon real or personal property
- Prosecute or defend claims against estate
- Sell, mortgage, or lease real or personal property
- Purchase real property

- Exercise options on insurance policies
- Operate a business on behalf of the person
- Buy or sell stocks, bonds, or securities
- Pay for the services of the guardian or attorneys

Staying Out of Trouble

The two areas in which the guardian of the estate is most likely to get into trouble involve commingling of funds and conflict of interest. While "never say never" is a well-recognized phrase, experienced guardians have some invaluable tips of things "never" to do:

- Never mix the guardian's money or investments with those of the person under guardianship, even if that person is a spouse. The person's assets must be kept in accounts in the guardianship's name using the person's Social Security number on the account.
- Never manage a guardianship estate so that the guardian or the guardian's family or friends profit from it or could even appear to profit. For example, the sale of the person's possessions to a family member for less than appraised value without court approval is a violation of the guardian's duty.
- Never borrow money or loan money to another person from the estate.
- Never give a gift from the estate without court approval.
- Never pay attorney's fees from the estate without court approval.
- Never pay guardian's fees from the estate without court approval.
- Never sell or dispose of real (and most personal) property without a court order (Standard 19.I).

9 Guardianship Modification

Terminating or Limiting the Guardianship

As each person's needs change throughout life, so does every guardianship evolve. The course of a guardianship is rarely static. In the initial phase after appointment, the guardian is occupied with investigating, researching, planning, and coordinating. As the guardianship proceeds, the guardian is more involved with monitoring, maintaining services, and managing assets. During the guardianship, the guardian must remain aware of all changes to the person's status. The need for adjustment to the plan of care and the management of the estate is continual. Eventually, the need for the guardianship will end, through changes and transitions in either the status of the person or the status of the guardian (Standard 21).

Terminating or limiting a guardianship always requires court action. The court terminates a guardianship upon:

- The person regaining capacity to manage his or her own affairs
- A minor person coming of age
- Appropriate alternatives to guardianship becoming available
- The death of the person
- The guardianship no longer benefits the person (Standard 21.III)

Changes in the Person's Status

The best possible transition occurs when the person regains capacity and is able to handle his or her own affairs. A change in guardianship is a very realistic and attainable goal for persons with medical conditions that can be brought under control, chemically dependent individuals who successfully complete treatment programs, accident victims who recover through rehabilitation or therapy, and individuals with intellectual disabilities who learn the skills to manage some aspects of their life or develop a system of supported decision making.

The guardian should be aware of indications that the person's decision-making abilities have improved and must assist the person in obtaining restoration of any appropriate legal rights (Standard 12.I.H).

For those individuals with the possibility of regaining capacity, the guardian should coordinate and carefully monitor a comprehensive program of therapies and activities designed to foster the person's independence and self-reliance (Ethical Principle 5). When it becomes evident that the person has the capacity to exercise some or all of the rights which were previously removed, a modification or revocation of the guardianship must occur. Reports from caregivers and evaluations from other professionals should be obtained to document the person's recovery of capacity. Where the guardian believes that the person has regained some or all decision-making capacity, the guardian has the affirmative duty to seek the limitation or termination of the guardianship through the court (Standard 2.VIII).

The person has the right to petition the court to modify or terminate the guardianship at any time. This includes the right to consult privately with legal counsel and other advocates to assist in this endeavor.

The guardian has an obligation to provide assistance and guidance to the person who seeks review of the guardianship, and in no way should hinder the person's attempts to exercise his or her rights. It is the court's decision, not the guardian's, as to whether the person needs continuing guardianship services. Restoration of some or all rights is a great indicator of the guardian's success in fostering the person's independence and self-reliance.

If the guardian does not agree that the guardianship should be limited or terminated and has obtained reports or evaluations that do not support restoration of the person's rights, the guardian should seek appointment of separate legal representation for the person (Standard 21).

In the event the court finds the person able to exercise one or more, but not all, of the rights that were removed, the court issues a new judgment, order, or letters of office stating the guardian's revised authority. In some states this, in effect, creates a new guardianship with new reporting duties and dates.

Minor Coming of Age

The need for guardianship of a minor terminates upon the child reaching majority, usually at age 18. Unless there is a reason to initiate an adult guardianship, assets held in the guardianship estate will be transferred to the individual. The guardian must complete all legal requirements to close a minor's guardianship.

Alternatives Become Available

A guardian's responsibilities may also be altered in the event a previously completed advance directive is discovered and can be successfully implemented. The guardian also should be aware of any services or supported decision making options that become available which would provide a less restrictive alternative to guardianship.

Death of the Person

If the guardian receives notice that the person's condition has deteriorated and death appears imminent, the guardian should notify the person's family and close friends as soon as possible. This will allow for their final visitation and to prepare them for the person's death. The guardian should notify every known family member even if they have not had recent contact with the person (Standard 4).

Guardians' duties technically cease upon the death of the person. In reality, the guardian may be called upon to assist with final arrangements, especially if there is no family or **personal representative**. The guardian of the property is usually required to pay funeral expenses and final medical bills, prepare and file with the court a final report and accounting, and transfer any remaining assets to the appropriate parties.

Ideally, burial or cremation plans would have been discussed with the person or the person's family far in advance of the need. Payment also could have been prearranged either by the person prior to the establishment of the guardianship or by the guardian as allowed by state law.

If the person did not make funeral arrangements, the guardian should be guided by directions outlined in the person's will, any advance directives, organ donation card, or wishes expressed to family members, friends, neighbors, or others when the person was still competent. Any arrangements, especially burial plots and grave markers, which were made at the time of the death of the person's spouse may provide guidance.

Collect and hold the person's personal belongings until it is determined who should receive them. The guardian should be prepared to transfer all personal papers and assets to the personal representative or executor of the person's estate. If no formal probate process is established, the papers and assets should be transferred to whomever the guardianship court directs. Be sure to get a dated, signed, and witnessed receipt, listing each item transferred.

Guardians are not officially discharged from their duties and surety bond until all legal requirements have been met. File a copy of the death certificate with the court and ask to be officially terminated as guardian. The guardian should determine how long state law requires that records and documents be retained after the termination of the guardianship.

Interstate Recognition

Each state's laws determine what **foreign guardians** appointed in another state can do when they need to transact business in another state. If a guardianship is initiated in one state and later the person needs to be moved to another state, perhaps to obtain treatment or to be closer to family members, or the guardian needs to sell real estate or collect a debt in another state, the guardian must adhere to the other state's laws. States that have adopted the Uniform Adult Guardianship and Protective

Proceedings Jurisdiction Act (UAGPPJA) have specific procedures that simplify the process to transfer a guardianship to another jurisdiction or have a guardian's authority recognized in another state.

Removal or Resignation of the Guardian

Proceedings to remove of the guardian may be initiated by the person, any **interested person**, the surety bond provider, or by the court on its own motion. Notice must be given to the guardian, and a hearing will be held to consider the petition and evidence.

Although state laws vary, the court may consider any of the following as reasons to remove the guardian:

- Fraud in obtaining the appointment
- Failure to perform duties
- Malfeasance, misfeasance, or nonfeasance
- Any incapacity or illness that renders the guardian incapable of discharging his or her duties
- Failure to comply with court orders
- Failure to use care and diligence in management of the person's estate
- Gross immorality
- Conviction of a felony
- Failure to obtain a bond when one is required
- Conflict of interest between the guardian and the person
- Failure to submit required reports in a timely manner

Whatever the reason, the guardianship is not terminated; rather, the status of the guardian is changed and a new guardian is appointed. The discharged guardian must file a final report and accounting and surrender all property and assets belonging to the person, as well as copies of all records pertaining to the guardianship.

Successor Guardianship

Changes in the guardian's status can also cause transitions in the guardianship. The guardian may resign, become ill, incapacitated, die, or be removed by the court for cause. Sometimes, a more appropriate person is identified to serve as guardian. Many public guardianship programs, for example, have an ongoing duty to seek a person of higher priority (such as a relative) to assume the responsibilities as guardian. In these situations, the guardianship does not end but is continued through the appointment of a successor guardian.

In some jurisdictions, a guardian is not permitted to resign until a successor guardian is available. If the guardian is unwilling or unable to continue in his or her duties, the guardian must submit to the court a notice of resignation and a petition for discharge. After being discharged, the guardian must complete a final report and accounting and transfer the person's assets, personal papers, and other significant information to the successor guardian.

The previous guardian should retain all documents and records pertaining to his or her actions. Successor guardians have a right to receive copies to ensure continuity in care and management.

RESOURCE MATERIALS

The following checklists and forms have been included as samples of some of the forms that guardians utilize. Please be sure to check with your state or court for any forms they may require you to use.

National Guardianship Association Resources
Initial New Guardianship Checklist
Functional Assessment for Guardianship Determination Form
Visitation in a Supported Environment Checklist
Medication Approval Checklist
Psychotropic Medication Approval Checklist
Treatment Approval Checklist
Marshal Estate Checklist
Budget Worksheet
Banking Institution Asset Inquiry Form
Inventory of Safe Deposit Box Form
Emergency Preparedness Checklist
Guardian's Personal Safety Checklist

NATIONAL GUARDIANSHIP ASSOCIATION RESOURCES

Education and Training Products

National Guardianship Association Standards of Practice

This must-have document covers NGA standards, including conflict of interest, decision making, medical services and medical treatment, management of the estate and the person, and more. Each standard is explained in detail and provides guidance to guardians in the private and public sector.

National Guardianship Association Ethical Principles

The NGA Ethical Principles are the condensed essence of the NGA Standards of Practice. The ten core principles are available on an easy-to-carry card for frequent reference.

Professional Development

Starting a Successful Guardianship Practice
Whether you are new to the guardianship field or need guidance with business issues, this manual is for you. It addresses issues such as business plans, business structure, insurance, marketing, licenses, taxes, and more.

Annual Legal and Legislative Review
Developed by attorneys and guardianship experts with more than 120 combined years of experience, the Legal and Legislative Review summarizes the major reported court decisions and legislation impacting guardianship during the past year. It contains abstracts of over a hundred court opinions and legislative enactments. Available in hardcopy or on a flash drive.

NGA Brochures

The National Guardianship Association offers seven brochures that explain in simple terms the basics of guardianship and a guardian's responsibilities in various situations.

Questions and Answers on Guardianship Issues
The Guardian and Informed Consent
The Guardian as Surrogate Decision-Maker
Guardianship/Conservatorship—An Overview
Guardianship of Persons with Intellectual Disabilities
Assisting the Guardian in Selecting a Care Facility
Rights of An Individual Under Guardianship

INITIAL NEW GUARDIANSHIP CHECKLIST

Person's Name: ____

Location: ____

Initials: ________________ Date Completed: ____________________

INTAKE AND ASSESSMENT

(Initial & Date)

________ / ________ Client Data Form

________ / ________ Initial Assessment

________ / ________ Photos of Client

________ / ________ Birthday Calendared

________ / ________ Mail Forwarding

________ / ________ Burial Information

________ / ________ Last Will and Testament dated: ____________________

________ / ________ Case Information Filed

________ / ________ Contact Information Filed

________ / ________ On Call Complete

COURT DOCUMENTS

________ / ________ Pleadings Obtained

________ / ________ Physician's Reports

________ / ________ Bond of Guardian: $ ____________________________

________ / ________ Bonding Company: ______________________________

________ / ________ Certified Letters of Guardianship (3 copies or more)

MEDICAL

________ / ________ Complete Report of Healthcare/Service Providers

________ / ________ Notify all Providers

________ / ________ Obtain Power of Attorney dated: ____________________

________ / ________ Obtain Living Will dated: ________________________

________ / ________ Obtain Health Care Surrogate Document dated: ________

________ / ________ Determine Code Status: ________________________

________ / ________ Confirm Medical Insurance Coverage

________ / ________ Obtain Copy of Medicare Card

________ / ________ Obtain Medicaid # ____________________________

________ / ________ Obtain Copy of Supplemental Insurance Card

________ / ________ Change Address for Medical Insurance(s)

________ / ________ Obtain Medical Records

________ / ________ Set up Medical Insurance Claims Procedure

________ / ________ Set up Emergency Preparedness

REAL PROPERTY

________ / ________ Complete Inspection N/A ________________________

________ / ________ Photos of Real Property N/A ______________________

________ / ________ Secure and Re-key Property (3 sets) N/A ____________

________ / ________ Create Maps and Directions to Real Property N/A ______

________ / ________ Schedule Appraisal on:______________ N/A _________

________ / ________ Arrange Lawn Maintenance N/A __________________

________ / ________ Schedule House Checks N/A _____________________

________ / ________ Verify Homeowner’s Insurance in Force: ______________

CLOTHING

________ / ________ Complete Clothing Inventory

PERSONAL PROPERTY

________ / ________ Photo Contents of Home date: ____________________

________ / ________ Video Contents of Home date: ____________________

Video Location: ____________________

________ / ________ Schedule Inventory and Appraisal of Contents on: ________

________ / ________ Verify Insurance of Personal Property: ____________________

________ / ________ Disposition of Personal Property date: ____________________

Details: ____________________

________ / ________ Re-Inventory of Moved Items date: ____________________

By: ____________________

Fine arts objects

________ / ________ Date/Description: ____________________

________ / ________ Date/Photos: ____________________

________ / ________ Date/Appraisal: ____________________

________ / ________ Date/Insurance: ____________________

________ / ________ Location: ____________________

Jewelry

________ / ________ Date/Description: ____________________

________ / ________ Date/Photos: ____________________

________ / ________ Date/Appraisal: ____________________

________ / ________ Date/Insurance: ____________________

________ / ________ Location: ____________________

Antiques

________ / ________ Date/Description: ______________________________

________ / ________ Date/Photos: ______________________________

________ / ________ Date/Appraisal: ______________________________

________ / ________ Date/Insurance: ______________________________

________ / ________ Location: ______________________________

Firearms

________ / ________ Date/Description: ______________________________

________ / ________ Date/Photos: ______________________________

________ / ________ Date/Appraisal: ______________________________

________ / ________ Date/Insurance: ______________________________

________ / ________ Location: ______________________________

Animals

________ / ________ Date/Description: ______________________________

________ / ________ Date/Photos: ______________________________

________ / ________ Location: ______________________________

VEHICLE(S)

________ / ________ Vehicle Intake Form N/A ______________________________

________ / ________ Auto Location: ______________________________

________ / ________ Verify Auto Insurance: ______________________________

________ / ________ Obtain Keys

________ / ________ Secure/Disable Vehicle by: ______________________________

________ / ________ Title Location: ______________________________

FINANCIAL

_________ / _________ Inventory Paperwork/Data Removed from Residence

_________ / _________ Research Assets

_________ / _________ Secure Bank Accounts

_________ / _________ Set up Guardianship Account

_________ / _________ Secure Brokerage Accounts

_________ / _________ Schedule Inventory of Safe Deposit Box on: ____________

_________ / _________ Schedule Social Security Appointment on: ____________

_________ / _________ Schedule Medicaid Application on: ____________

_________ / _________ Transfer All Income Benefits to Guardianship Account

_________ / _________ Change Address for Utilities

_________ / _________ Obtain Prior Tax Returns

_________ / _________ Confirm Life Insurance: ____________

_________ / _________ Cancel Credit Cards

_________ / _________ Confirm Benefits Eligibility

_________ / _________ Prepare Initial Budget

REFERRAL

_________ / _________ Referral Source: ____________

_________ / _________ Thank You Sent

OTHER RESPONSIBILITIES

_________ / _________ ____________

_________ / _________ ____________

_________ / _________ ____________

FUNCTIONAL ASSESSMENT FOR GUARDIANSHIP DETERMINATION

Name: ______________________________ Date: ______ / ______ / ______

Facility's Name: ________________________ Case Number: ____________

Disability Category: ☐ ID ☐ MI ☐ DA ☐ PH DOB ________ Age _____

Level of Care ____

Provide a brief explanation of the individual's background. (i.e., When and why was this person admitted to an institutional facility?)

____

____

____

Current Diagnosis: ____

____

MEDICAL STATUS

Attending Physician: ____

☐ Dental ☐ Eye ☐ Physical ______ / ______ / ______

Date of Last Visit: ______ / ______ / ______ Current Weight: ____________

Diet: ____

Ideal Body Weight: ____

Current Medications/Treatment: ___________________________________

____

____

____

Most Recent Medical Problems Treated; Lab Work/Consultations/Hospitalizations

____

____

____

____

____

____

____

____

____

Assessment of Functional Skills

For the skill areas that follow, please check all statements which accurately describe this individual. Where deficits are found, provide a brief explanation as to how this interferes with the individual making an informed consent regarding his or her care, treatment, placement, or financial matters. Be specific!

A. BEHAVIOR

- ☐ Relates well to others
- ☐ Becomes suspicious or quarrelsome with little or no provocation
- ☐ Has inappropriate and/or repetitive movements (Give examples)

____

____

____

How does the above marked item(s) interfere with the person making an informed consent to care, treatment, placement, or management of financial affairs?

____

____

____

B. RECEPTIVE COMMUNICATION

- ☐ Can understand and remember complex instructions for 24-hour period.
- ☐ Understands simple two-step directions (greater than 1 hour).
- ☐ Understands simple one-step directions, but quickly forgets them.
- ☐ Does not appear to understand verbal communication, but does respond to gestures.
- ☐ Does not appear to understand simple gestures (i.e. sit down, come here, etc.)

How does the above marked item(s) interfere with the person making an informed consent to care, treatment, placement, or management of financial affairs?

____

____

____

C. EXPRESSIVE COMMUNICATION

- ☐ Carries on complex conversation involving abstract ideas
- ☐ Carries on simple conversation involving routine matters
- ☐ Uses two word sentences
- ☐ Uses monosyllables or gestures (circle one)
- ☐ Able to converse, but is off subject area

How does the above marked item(s) interfere with the person making an informed consent to care, treatment, placement, or management of financial affairs?

____

____

____

D. WRITTEN COMMUNICATION

Briefly describe this person's ability to read, write, and understand simple mathematics. Please include whether or not he/she understands the concept of money.

____

____

____

____

If there is a deficit in written communication skills, briefly explain how this interferes with the person's ability to provide an informed consent to care, treatment, placement, or management of financial affairs.

____

____

____

E. ORIENTATION

- ☐ Is living in the present and is aware of his or her present condition
- ☐ Is orientated to his or her environment
- ☐ Knows names of significant others (i.e. family, friends, staff, etc.)
- ☐ Knows and responds to own name
- ☐ Needs simple reality orientation (i.e. being reminded of day, where he or she is, etc.)
- ☐ Can function without institutional routine (i.e. knows when & where to eat, dresses appropriately, can find bedroom, dining area, bath, etc.)
- ☐ Needs to be led from place to place
- ☐ Is completely unresponsive to his/her environment

If the person is not in contact with reality or somewhat disorientated, please describe his or her orientation. Give examples.

____

____

____

F. HEALTH CARE

- ☐ Knows when he/she has a health concern
- ☐ Will express need for medical or dental services
- ☐ Lets appropriate people know if there is a health problem
- ☐ Is reliable in taking medication
- ☐ Can self-medicate
- ☐ Requires assistance in keeping medical appointments (i.e. needs reminders, help in transportation arrangements, etc.)
- ☐ Is able to indicate verbally, or by gesture if in pain

How does the above marked item(s) interfere with the person making an informed consent to care, treatment, placement, or management of financial affairs?

____

____

____

G. CONSENT TO MEDICAL CARE

- ☐ Is able to exercise an informed choice about medical treatment
- ☐ Is able to make a voluntary choice about medical treatment
- ☐ Understands he/she is free to choose or refuse medical treatments
- ☐ Understands possible consequences of choice
- ☐ Has a lay person's understanding and is able to discuss possible risks involved in suggested medical treatment
- ☐ Will go along with whatever medical treatment is suggested.

If the person is unable to exercise the above aspects of informed medical consent, please describe how the individual responds when medical consent is needed.

____

____

____

Scope of Guardianship

Please indicate those areas where you feel this person is unable to exercise informed consent. This listing should act as your guide for determining the scope of limited versus plenary guardianship.

- ☐ Decisions concerning travel (i.e., ability to move about in community)
- ☐ Consent to medical or other professional care, counseling, treatment
- ☐ Access to and refusal or consent to release confidential records
- ☐ Management of personal money
- ☐ Entering contracts (leasing agreements, payment for services rendered, etc.)
- ☐ Requesting advocacy or legal services, if needed
- ☐ Making gifts or charitable contributions
- ☐ Decisions concerning education, employment, or day treatment
- ☐ Voluntary admission to hospital, or other treatment facility when necessary
- ☐ Other (list and explain) ____________________________

____

____

____

Does this person have friends or family who can assist him or her on a regular basis? If not, please state whether or not they have the ability to seek assistance from others to compensate for their deficit areas.

____

____

____

____

____

Based on this assessment, I believe guardianship is in this person's best interest in the following areas:

- ☐ Daily Care
- ☐ Medical Treatment
- ☐ Placement Determination
- ☐ Management of Personal Finances

Prospective Guardians

____

____

____

Describe the nature of contact (visits, telephone calls, letters) involved persons have had with this person over the past two years. ________________

____

____

____

____

Worker Signature: ____________________

Name/Title of Person Providing Information: ________________ How long have you known this individual? ________ / ________ / ________

VISITATION IN A SUPPORTED ENVIRONMENT CHECKLIST

Client's Name: ______________________________

Today's Date: ______________________________

1. Hygiene/Appearance

   - ☐ Fit, condition, cleanliness, and style of clothing

____

____

____

   - ☐ Hair—style and cleanliness

____

____

____

   - ☐ Nails trimmed/clean

____

____

____

   - ☐ Utilizing adaptive devices—eyeglasses, hearing aids, dentures

____

____

____

   - ☐ Access to personal hygiene supplies of choosing

____

____

____

2. Environment

- ☐ Clean/odor-free

- ☐ Home like

- ☐ Personalized

- ☐ Accessible

- ☐ Adequate furnishings

- ☐ Adequate clothing

3. Life/Safety

☐ Accessible emergency exits

____

____

____

☐ Evacuation plan

____

____

____

☐ Smoke detectors or sprinklers

____

____

____

☐ Hazardous chemicals controlled

____

____

____

4. Interpersonal Interactions with Staff

☐ Respectful/nurturing

____

____

____

☐ Age appropriate

____

____

____

☐ People first language

5. Appropriate Activities

☐ Functional

☐ Based on individual preference

☐ Evidence of choice

6. General Health Status

☐ Best possible health

☐ Change in health status

☐ Preventative health care

7. Miscellaneous

☐ Menu of meals provided

☐ Towels/linens

☐ Locked areas—who has access?

☐ Weekend routine—how is religious preference addressed

☐ If roommate—do they get along?

- ☐ Access to privacy, phone, mail

8. Medical Record Review
   - ☐ What to look for
   - ☐ What to record
9. Program Record/Documentation
   - ☐ Weekly activity schedule
   - ☐ Community integration opportunities
   - ☐ Restriction

☐ Progress notes

____

____

____

☐ Program data

____

____

____

____

Signature of Guardian

MEDICATION APPROVAL CHECKLIST

Client's Name: ____

Today's Date: ____

Diagnosis: ____

____

Symptoms: ____

____

Proposed Treatment: ____

____

____

Name of Medication: ____

Expected outcome: ____

Dosage: ____

Duration: ____

Possible Allergic Reactions: ____

____

Possible Drug Interactions: ____

____

Possible Side Effects: ____

____

Special Considerations (dietary, time for administrations): ____________________

____

____

____

Notes: ____

____

____

____

____

____

____

Signature of Guardian

PSYCHOTROPIC MEDICATION APPROVAL CHECKLIST

Client's Name: ____

Today's Date: ____

Diagnosis: ____

____

Symptoms: ____

____

Proposed Treatment: ____

____

____

Proposed Medication: ____

PHASE 1: ASSESSMENT

1. Specific diagnosis is defined. ☐
2. Target behavior(s) or symptoms are defined in specific and observable terms. ☐
3. A data collection method is specified. (frequency count, duration recording, time sample, interval recording, rating scale, permanent product, or some combination thereof) ☐
4. Baseline data is available for comparison (2- to 4-week period if possible). ☐
5. Consider psychosocial and environmental factors and causes. ☐
6. Consider organic, medical/illness, and other drug factors and causes, ☐
7. Review previous psychotropic and behavioral interventions. ☐
8. Review any active treatment programs. ☐

PHASE 2: TREATMENT PLAN

1. The proposed psychotropic medication is specified. ☐
2. Dose and dose range are specified and are within the limit for age or population group. ☐
3. Frequency and route of administration are specified. ☐
4. Possible side effects are specified and a written copy of these possible side effects is provided. ☐
5. The following do not occur (Note: there may be exceptions but

they need to be strongly documented. The exceptions are not typically found with first time episodes or new plans; rather, they usually occur with repeated failure) ☐

A. Use of two drugs from the same class
B. Use of three drugs or more at the same time from any class
C. Sedative hypnotic use for more than short periods of time

6. Effectiveness or ineffectiveness of the medication is defined by a specified improvement level compared to the baseline. ☐
7. Consider options if the specific medication does not have desired effect. ☐
8. Consider adverse effects on positive behavior. ☐
9. An active treatment plan is in place (exception for dementia). ☐
10. The method and timeline to check for side effects is specified (including a scale and timeline to check for tardive dyskinesia with antipsychotics). ☐
11. Client is included in plan as much as possible. ☐

PHASE 3: MONITORING

1. Data is collected on target behaviors using specified method. ☐
2. Data indicate the drug is having its intended effect. ☐
3. Review formal psychotropic medication regimen at least quarterly with appropriate interdisciplinary team participation. ☐
4. Monitor for side effects at least quarterly (including a tardive dyskinesia exam at least once every six months with antipsychotics). ☐
5. Consider adverse impact on functional capacity or ability to perform life functions. ☐
6. Review at three and six months after initiation for continued use. ☐
7. Review PRN (as needed) monthly. ☐
8. Attempt periodic gradual reductions to determine if the psychotropic is still required if possible. ☐
9. Continue active treatment programs if appropriate. ☐
10. Review and consent to any dose or program changes. ☐
11. Renew consent in writing at least once per year. ☐
12. Renew consent in writing for all changes outside the approved dosage range. ☐

____

Signature of Guardian

TREATMENT APPROVAL CHECKLIST

Client's Name: ______________________________

Today's Date: ______________________________

Diagnosis: ______________________________

____

Symptoms: ______________________________

____

Proposed Treatment: ______________________________

____

____

Diagnosis or targeted behavior: ______________________________

____

____

____

Baseline data: ______________________________

____

____

____

Proposed treatment, procedure, or intervention: ______________________________

____

____

____

Expected Outcome: ______________________________

____

____

____

Expected duration of treatment: ______________________________________

____

____

____

Anticipated effect on daily life: ______________________________________

____

____

____

Possible complications or risks: ______________________________________

____

____

____

Care required after procedure or treatment: ____________________________

____

____

____

Second opinion requested: ____

Person's ability to participate: _______________________________________

____

____

____

Staff qualification to provide treatment: ______________________________

____

____

____

Program evaluation (method/dates): ___________________________________

____

____

Determination of success: ____

____

____

____

____

Signature of Guardian

MARSHAL ESTATE CHECKLIST

Client's Name: ____

Today's Date: ____

- ☐ Obtain certified letters of office
- ☐ Redirect mail
- ☐ Secure property (change locks, board up)
- ☐ Notify interested parties of appointment
- ☐ Close charge accounts (in writing)
- ☐ Check motor vehicle registration for ownership
- ☐ Check ownership of real property
- ☐ List assets, income sources, and liabilities
- ☐ Determine income tax status (old returns)
- ☐ Locate bank statements, checks, check registers
- ☐ Apply for Representative Payee
- ☐ Apply for eligible benefits
- ☐ Obtain copy of will
- ☐ Assess adequacy of insurance coverage on automobiles
- ☐ Assess adequacy of insurance coverage on houses
- ☐ Determine health insurance coverage
- ☐ Inventory contents of residence (with witness)
- ☐ Secure personal property
- ☐ Gather and review personal papers
- ☐ Clean out residence
- ☐ Check property tax status
- ☐ Locate banking institutions
- ☐ Assess ownership of accounts
- ☐ Close accounts (be mindful of joint or POD accounts)
- ☐ Open new guardianship account(s)
- ☐ Inventory safe deposit box (with witness) and close
- ☐ File court required inventory

BUDGET WORKSHEET

Client Name: ________________ Effective Date: ______ / ______ / ______

Approval Date: ______ / ______ / ______

Guardian Administered Income:

SSI	$ ____________
SSDI	$ ____________
TANF	$ ____________
Wages Deposited into Guardianship Account	$ ____________
Other Sources of Income (Specify)	$ ____________
TOTAL MONTHLY INCOME EXPECTED	$ ____________

Expenses:

Rent	$ ____________
Phone	$ ____________
Gas	$ ____________
Electric	$ ____________
Food	$ ____________
Spending	$ ____________
Water/Sewage	$ ____________
Cable	$ ____________
Transportation	$ ____________
Credit card payments	$ ____________
Installment payments	$ ____________
Other	$ ____________
Service Charge	$ ____________
TOTAL MONTHLY EXPENSES EXPECTED	$ ____________

Balance At End of Month:

Checking Acct: Balance: $ ______________ Date: _____ / _____ / _____

Savings Acct: Balance: $ ______________ Date: _____ / _____ / _____

**Does individual agree with Budget?* ☐ Yes ☐ No

If "NO," individual's input: ______________________________

____

____

If client is not receiving full benefit amount entitled to, please explain (overpayment: total amount, monthly reduction amount, time frame; or reduced benefits due to earnings, etc.)

____

____

Explanation of Budget/Financial Plan:

____

____

PERSONAL AND FINANCIAL INFORMATION

1. Client: ______________ Date of Birth: _____ / _____ / _____
2. **Guardian Administered Bank Accounts:**

Checking Bank: ______________ Acct #: ______________

Address: ______________ Earns Interest/Amt: ______________

Saving Bank: ______________ Acct #: ______________

Address: ______________ Earns Interest/Amt: ______________

Other: ______________________________

Personal Accounts:

Savings: ________ Checking: ________ Acct #: ________ Acct Bal: ________

Account Name: ______________ Bank Name: ______________

Bank Address: ______________________________

3. Benefits:

SS#: ________-________-________ SSI Claim #: ______________________________

SSDI Claim#: ___________________________ Other Claim #'s: ___________________

Medicare #: _____________________ Is Premium Deducted from SSDI: ☐ Yes ☐ No

Medicaid#: ______________________ Spend down: ☐ Yes ☐ No

Amt: __________ Redet Date: __________ Medicaid Recipient #: ______________

Food Stamp #: ________________ Amt: ____________ Redet Date: _____________

ADC #: ________________ Amt: ________________ Redet Date: ________________

Other Benefit/Assistance (liheap, energy credits) ______________________________

4. Insurance:

Prepaid Funeral Contract: ☐ Yes ☐ No Amt: ________ Contract #: _________

Name of Policy: ____

Name of Funeral Home/Address: ____

Life Ins. Policy: ☐ Yes ☐ No Company: ____________ Policy #: ____________

Policy Amt: ____________ Face Value: ____________ Cash in Value: ____________

Policy Owner: ______________________ Name of Insured: ____________________

Beneficiary: _______________________ Location of Policy: ___________________

Other Insurance Company: ________________________ Policy #: ________________

Type of Coverage: ________________________ Amount: _______________________

5. Real Estate / Property Assets:

____

____

____

RESIDENTIAL INFORMATION

6. Address:

Client Mailing Address: ____________ Home Address (If different) ____________

______________________________ ______________________________

______________________________ ______________________________

______________________________ ______________________________

______________________________ ______________________________

7. All Utilities:

Company Acct#. Budget Amt.

____

____

____

____

8. Rent:

Landlord: ____________ Date Due: _____ / _____ / _____ Amt Due: ________

Payee: ________________________ Check Memo: ____________________

Mailing Address: ____________ Rent or Rm & Bd? Deposit pd/amt: ________

________________________ Late Charge: __________ Late After: ________

________________________ Subsidized Housing: ☐ Yes ☐ No

________________________ Has Client Signed Lease: ☐ Yes ☐ No

________________________ Does Rep have copy of lease: ☐ Yes ☐ No

Term of Lease: ☐ Month to Month ☐ 6 Months ☐ 1 Year ☐ Other

9. Household (*if spouse, list date of marriage)

Name each Individual in Household other than Client	Adult or Minor A or M	Relationship to Client	Source of Income
1.			
2.			
3.			
4.			
5.			

SCHEDULED CHECKS

10. (Utilities do not need to be listed here unless installment payments)

☐ Payee: ______________ Amt: _____________ Mail Date: _____ / _____ / _____

Send to Clients Mailing Address: Yes/No Check Memo: ____________________

If No, specify address: __________________

______________________________________ Installment Payment ☐ Yes ☐ No

______________________________________ Account #: ____________________

______________________________________ Current Balance Due: ___________

______________________________________ Projected "Pay off" Date: ________

☐ Payee: ______________ Amt: _____________ Mail Date: _____ / _____ / _____

Send to Clients Mailing Address: Yes/No Check Memo: ____________________

If No, specify address: __________________

______________________________________ Installment Payment ☐ Yes ☐ No

______________________________________ Account #: ____________________

______________________________________ Current Balance Due: ___________

______________________________________ Projected "Pay off" Date: ________

☐ Payee: ______________ Amt: _____________ Mail Date: _____ / _____ / _____

Send to Clients Mailing Address: Yes/No Check Memo: ____________________

If No, specify address: __________________

______________________________________ Installment Payment ☐ Yes ☐ No

________________ Account #: __________

________________ Current Balance Due: __________

________________ Projected “Pay off” Date: __________

☐ Payee: ________ Amt: ________ Mail Date: ____ / ____ / ____

Send to Clients Mailing Address: Yes/No Check Memo: __________

If No, specify address: __________

________________ Installment Payment ☐ Yes ☐ No

________________ Account #: __________

________________ Current Balance Due: __________

________________ Projected “Pay off” Date: __________

☐ Payee: ________ Amt: ________ Mail Date: ____ / ____ / ____

Send to Clients Mailing Address: Yes/No Check Memo: __________

If No, specify address: __________

________________ Installment Payment ☐ Yes ☐ No

________________ Account #: __________

________________ Current Balance Due: __________

________________ Projected “Pay off” Date: __________

EARNED INCOME INFORMATION SHEET

11. (Complete only if applicable)

Monthly Gross Amount: ____________________

Place of Employment: ____________________

Address/Phone/Contact Person: ____________________

____

____

Wages received: Yes/No Frequency: ________________

Earnings reported monthly to Soc. Sec. By ________________*

Does employer also report earnings to Soc. Sec.? ☐ Yes ☐ No

Does client have a tax exempt status (W4)? ☐ Yes ☐ No

Monthly breakdown of previous 12 months gross earned income:

Month / Year	Amount

Month / Year	Amount

For SSDI Recipients:

1. Has individual completed the 9 month *"Trial Work Period"? ☐ Yes ☐ No
2. If #1 is "yes", has Social Security reviewed the individuals **Substantial Gainful Activity Status? ☐ Yes ☐ No
3. Is this person at the SGA lever, according to Social Security? ☐ Yes ☐ No

BANKING INSTITUTION ASSET INQUIRY FORM

Date: _____ / _____ / _____

Client name: ________________________________

We are in the process of determining the assets for the above mentioned. We are requesting the following information be completed for all accounts that may be held with your institution. A self-addressed envelope is enclosed for your reply.

Banking Institution:	Bank Address:

CHECKING AND SAVINGS ACCOUNT(S)

Type of Account				
Acct. No.				
Titling of Account				
Date Opened				
Date Closed				
Closed by Whom				
Interest Rate				
Balance as of / /				
Current balance				

Are there any Direct Deposits being made to the above account(s)?
If so, which one(s) and from where?

SAFE DEPOSIT BOX

Box No., & Titling of Box		
Date Opened		
Date Closed		
Closed by Whom		

CERTIFICATES OF DEPOSITS

Certificate No & Titling of Certificate		
Date Opened		
Maturity Date		
Closed by Whom		
Current Balance: As of / /		
Term of CD & Rate:		

MISC. ACCOUNTS

Type of Account		
Acct. # & Titling		
Date Opened and Closed		
Closed by Whom		
Current Balance: As of / /		

Any additional information or comments concerning investments or transactions which you may have had with the above person will be appreciated. Please list or attach a separate sheet.

____ /_____ /_____

Completed by Title Phone # Date

INVENTORY OF SAFE DEPOSIT BOX FORM

______________________ (the guardian's name), the guardian of the property of ______________________, files this inventory of the contents of safe deposit box number______________________ located at (name and address of institution)

____

on ____________________, ____________________, conducted in the presence of ______________________, an employee of the above-named institution.

CASH (U.S. Currency) $______________________.__________

COINS, ETC. OTHER THAN STANDARD U.S. CURRENCY

Description: ____

____

____

STOCKS, BONDS, SECURITIES

Name Description Number of Each

____

____

COLLECTIBLES

Description: ____

____

____

OTHER PERSONAL PROPERTY

Description: ____

____

____

OTHER DOCUMENTS OR ITEMS

Will ________________________ Dated ________________

Social Security Card ________________________________

Birth Certificate ___________________________________

Deeds:

Description or Address of Property __________________

____

____

Trust Documents: ____________________________________

____

____

Other: ____

____

____

OTHER

Description: ____

____

____

The above-described safe deposit box contained no other items of any kind.

Under penalties of perjury, I declare that I have read the foregoing, and the facts alleged are true, to the best of my knowledge and belief.

Executed this ________________ day of ____________, ________

____

Guardian

I verify that I, an employee of ____________________________________
was present during the opening of the above-described safe deposit box and that I witnessed the inventory of its contents, and I verify that the above inventory is accurate and correct.

____

Witness Name

Address:

____

____

____

Phone Number:

____

EMERGENCY PREPAREDNESS CHECKLIST

Client: ____

Date Requested: ______ / ______ / ______

______ Residence ________ Mobile Home Located at: ______________

____

____________ Storage Unit # ____________ Located at: ______________

____

Weatherization In Anticipation of Hurricane

Special Attention:

______ Move garbage cans, awnings and other large outdoor items inside home or garage

______ Place protective covering over windows and garage doors

______ Garage or store vehicles if on property

______ Moor boats securely

______ Shut off water, electricity, and gas

______ If there is a swimming pool, cover the pump filter

______ If the residence is a manufactured home, secure tie-downs

______ Trim loose or hanging tree limbs

Date: ____________________

Notes: ____

____

____

____

____

____

Other Preparation Steps

- ☐ Verify type and amount of insurance on real and personal property
- ☐ Confirm that insurance coverage includes natural disasters, including hurricanes, floods, sinkholes
- ☐ Determine evacuation plan
- ☐ Prepare "grab and go" evacuation kit with flashlight, battery TV, battery radio, batteries, cash, area map, directions to evacuation site, first aid kit, extra prescription drugs, hearing aid batteries, extra pair of glasses, phone charger
- ☐ Place important papers in waterproof/fireproof box
- ☐ Prepare disaster preparation box with COPIES of Social Security card, passport, driver's license, Medicare card, health insurance card, medical records, birth certificates, credit cards, insurance policies, financial records, some blank checks
- ☐ List emergency contacts; account numbers with creditors, banks, and brokers; prescription drugs with dosage and frequency
- ☐ Arrange a phone tree of persons to call in the event of evacuation
- ☐ Make plans for care of pets

Date:

____

Print

____

Signature

Reference: State Farm Insurance Hurricane Awareness Brochure and FEMA

POST STORM EVALUATION

(Evaluation should take place within 24 hours after the hurricane threat is over and it is safe to return to the property)

Date: ____________________

Client: ____________________________

Damage to: ________________________ Photos taken

_____ Lawn Furniture _____ Tie-Downs (mobile homes) _____ Windows

_____ Roof _____ Shattered Glass _____ Pool

Notes: ____

____

____

____

____

____

____

____

____

____

Date: ____________________

____

Print

____

Signature

GUARDIAN'S PERSONAL SAFETY CHECKLIST

Persons subject to guardianship or their family members may become angry or belligerent. Remember to take necessary precautions to protect yourself whether in the office or in the community and consider each of the following precautions when going about your work:

In All Situations

- ☐ Be aware of your surroundings. Increase your awareness and vigilance of what is happening around you.
- ☐ Follow your instincts. If a situation feels threatening, leave or seek assistance.

Personal Safety Tips

- ☐ Wear comfortable clothing and shoes that allow you to move.
- ☐ Do not expose expensive jewelry, money, or the contents of your purse or bag.
- ☐ Be cautious with personal information.
- ☐ Keep personal and office keys with you.
- ☐ Keep your wallet, purse, or other valuables with you or in a locked desk or file cabinet drawer.

Meeting People In Your Workplace

- ☐ Keep the door ajar.
- ☐ Sit close to the door.
- ☐ Be sure someone else is in the office.
- ☐ Meet in a space closer to activity, if your office is isolated.
- ☐ Make sure another staff member knows you are meeting with someone.
- ☐ Avoid making appointments at the end of the day or week with individuals known to be difficult.
- ☐ Keep your desktop clear of any objects that might be used as a weapon.
- ☐ Keep a solid object (desk) between you and the individual.

Working Late

- ☐ Avoid working alone after hours.
- ☐ Tell someone when and where to expect you.
- ☐ Lock doors; check washrooms, and storage areas while others are still present.
- ☐ Avoid isolated stairwells and restrooms.
- ☐ Proceed cautiously when leaving.
- ☐ Request an escort to your car.

In The Field

- ☐ Carry a cell phone.
- ☐ Take someone with you—another staff person, case manager, etc.
- ☐ Make sure someone knows where you are and your itinerary.
- ☐ Carry as little as possible.

Working With Angry Individuals

To ignore the anger of an individual is to ignore the threat to personal safety. Subtle signs of anger include:

- ☐ Rapid respiration
- ☐ Pupils dilated
- ☐ Fixed stare
- ☐ Bunching up of the body/clenching of fists
- ☐ Voice or complexion change
- ☐ Facial expressions

Some individuals may exhibit unpredictable behavior due to mental illness or a brain injury. The following are some warning signs that a person may become violent:

- ☐ Resists change
- ☐ Is sullen, angry, or depressed
- ☐ Identifies with or praises acts of violence
- ☐ Recently obtained a weapon
- ☐ Threatens, intimidates, or manipulates others
- ☐ Thinks others are out to get him/her
- ☐ Over reacts to criticism
- ☐ Blames others for their own mistakes
- ☐ Has had recent police encounters
- ☐ Has a history of assault
- ☐ Others are afraid of or apprehensive about this person

Use specific verbal and non-verbal tools to maintain calm in a tense situation:

- ☐ Use a quieter voice; however, remember that a sudden loud voice that startles an aggressor may buy you some time if that becomes necessary.
- ☐ Use a commanding voice, not a questioning voice.
- ☐ Maintain distance.

- ☐ Do not turn your back.
- ☐ Use a diffuse kind of eye contact—look at the face to shoulders area rather than directly in the eyes.
- ☐ Show support and empathy, do not argue.
- ☐ Be firm and set limits.
- ☐ Set firm ground rules for future contract.

APPENDIX

APPENDIX A

National Guardianship Association Ethical Principles

1. A guardian treats the person with dignity. (Standard 3)
2. A guardian involves the person to the greatest extent possible in all decision making. (Standard 9)
3. A guardian selects the option that places the least restrictions on the person's freedom and rights. (Standard 8)
4. A guardian identifies and advocates for the person's goals, needs, and preferences. (Standard 7)
5. A guardian maximizes the self-reliance and independence of the person. (Standard 9)
6. A guardian keeps confidential the affairs of the person. (Standard 11)
7. A guardian avoids conflicts of interest and self-dealing. (Standard 16)
8. A guardian complies with all laws and court orders. (Standard 2)
9. A guardian manages all financial matters carefully. (Standard 18)
10. A guardian respects that the money and property being managed belongs to the person. (Standard 17)

The term "guardian" includes all court-appointed fiduciaries. These Ethical Principles are reflected throughout the National Guardianship Association *Standards of Practice*. Guardians should look to the *Standards* for guidance on ways to carry out these ethical principles, with specific reference to the highlighted standards.

APPENDIX B

National Guardianship Association Standards of Practice

Preamble

Developing standards for guardians has been an ongoing challenge for the National Guardianship Association (NGA). Not only has the profession undergone rapid change since the original seven standards were written in 1991, but the basic issues have been, and remain, imprecise and difficult to define for a national, membership-based organization. A basic philosophical element complicating the process has been the need to strike a consistent balance between standards that represent an ideal and those that recognize practical limitations, whether for a family guardian or for a professional guardian.

In July of 1991, the NGA adopted a previously published Model Code of Ethics to guide guardians in their decision-making process. The next task of the NGA was to formulate specific standards to be applied in the day-to-day practice of guardianship. The seven original standards of practice that were written and adopted by the NGA in 1991 have now been expanded to cover more of the duties and responsibilities that face court-appointed guardians today.

The same lengthy discussions that took place in 1991 occurred again during each updating of the standards. These discussions centered on the need to state what is "right" versus the need to recognize and accept the inevitability of the status quo—too many clients, not enough funding or staff. While we all agree that such restrictions are all too commonplace, we also feel that little is gained by simply accepting a substandard or unacceptable state of affairs. NGA has, therefore, adopted standards that we feel reflect as realistically as possible the best or highest quality of practice. In many cases, best practice may go beyond what state law requires of a guardian.

In reading this document, it is important to recognize that some of the standards enunciate ideals or philosophical points, while others speak to day-to-day practical matters. Both approaches are critically important. It is not our ambition to prescribe a precise program description or management manual. Rather, we have sought to shape a mirror that practitioners can use to evaluate their efforts. The standards also reflect the mandate that all guardians must perform in accordance with current state law governing guardianships and certification of guardians.

To ensure consistency in the way the standards are applied, the following constructions are used: "shall" imposes a duty, "may" creates discretionary authority or grants permission or a power, "must" creates or recognizes a condition precedent, "is entitled to" creates or recognizes a right, and "may not" imposes a prohibition and is synonymous with "shall not." The guidelines that appear in some standards are suggested ways of carrying out those standards.

This document embodies practices and standards from a number of professional sources. As such, it sometimes makes unavoidable use of legal and medical "terms of art" where they would commonly and most accurately be used by professionals who work in the particular area. In addition, the field of guardianship itself makes use of terms that vary widely from state to state. "Guardian" and "person under guardianship" or "person" are the terms used here to simplify the many references to these roles. Where points apply to professional (as opposed to family) guardians, they are indicated. "Guardian," as used in the standards, means guardian of the person, guardian of the estate, or guardian of the person and estate, depending on the standard being addressed.

In this work, we have drawn on a number of collective sources. First and foremost have been NGA members who have contributed extensive time and energy and valuable input into the development of these standards. The *Model Code of Ethics for Guardians*, developed by Michael D. Casasanto, Mitchell Simon, and Judith Roman and adopted by the NGA, formed the foundation from which the standards were developed. Other very important sources that helped in the creation of our standards of practice are the U.S. Administration on Aging (now a part of the Administration on Community Living), the AARP, the Center for Social Gerontology, the Michigan Offices of Services for the Aging, and the state guardianship associations for Arizona, California, Illinois, Michigan, Minnesota, and Washington. We thank all those who have contributed to the development of these Standards for their ongoing commitment to the profession of guardianship.

The *NGA Standards of Practice for Guardians* were first adopted by the NGA Board of Directors and ratified by the membership in 2000. The 2003 edition of the *Standards* incorporated language that came forth from Wingspan 2001, the National Conference on Guardianship Reform. The 2007 edition provided minor clarification of the language in the earlier editions without any substantive changes. These standards were used as a starting point by the 2011 Third National Guardianship Summit in developing new standards. The 2013 edition incorporates the recommendations of this Summit. In 2016 NGA adopted *Ethical Principles* which highlight the core principles found throughout the standards.

Please be advised that any entity adopting these standards should give attribution to NGA.

Check the NGA Website (www.guardianship.org) for the most current edition of the *NGA Standards of Practice* and the *Ethical Principles*.

NGA Standards of Practice

NGA Standard 1—Applicable Law and General Standards

I. The guardian shall perform duties and discharge obligations in accordance with current state and federal law governing guardianships.

II. The guardian who is certified, registered, or licensed by the Center for Guardianship Certification or by his or her state should be guided by professional codes of ethics and standards of practice for guardians.

III. In all guardianships, the guardian shall comply with the requirements of the court that made the appointment.

IV. Every guardian should be held to the same standards, regardless of familial relationship, except a guardian with a higher level of relevant skills shall be held to the use of those skills.

NGA Standard 2—The Guardian's Relationship to the Court

I. The guardian shall know the extent of the powers and the limitations of authority granted by the court and all decisions and actions shall be consistent with that court order.

II. The guardian shall obtain court authorization for actions that are subject to court approval.

III. The guardian shall clarify with the court any questions about the meaning of the order or directions from the court before taking action based on the order or directions.

IV. The guardian shall seek assistance as needed to fulfill responsibilities to the person under guardianship.

V. All payments to the guardian from the assets of the person shall follow applicable federal or state statutes, rules, and requirements and are subject to review by the court.

VI. The guardian shall submit reports regarding the status of the guardianship to the court as ordered by the court or required by state statute, but no less often than annually. Ways that guardians of the person and of the estate keep the court informed about the well-being of the person and the status of the estate include but not limited to:

   A. Personal care plans and financial plans,
   B. Inventories and appraisals, and
   C. Reports and accountings.

VII. The guardian shall use available technology to:

   A. File the general plan, inventory and appraisal, and annual reports and accountings,

B. Access responsible education and information about guardianships, and
C. Assist in the administration of the estate.

VIII. The guardian shall promptly inform the court of any change in the capacity of the person that warrants an expansion or restriction of the guardian's authority.

NGA Standard 3—The Guardian's Professional Relationship with the Person

I. The guardian shall treat the person under guardianship with dignity.
II. The guardian shall avoid personal relationships with the person, the person's family, or the person's friends, unless the guardian is a family member, or unless such a relationship existed before the appointment of the guardian.
III. The guardian may not engage in sexual relations with a person unless the guardian is the person's spouse or in a physical relationship that existed before the appointment of the guardian.
IV. The guardian shall seek ongoing education concerning the following:

A. Person-centered planning,
B. Surrogate decision-making,
C. Responsibilities and duties of guardians,
D. Legal processes of guardianship, and
E. State certification of guardians.

NGA Standard 4—The Guardian's Relationship with Family Members and Friends of the Person

I. The guardian shall promote social interactions and meaningful relationships consistent with the preferences of the person under guardianship.

A. The guardian shall encourage and support the person in maintaining contact with family and friends, as defined by the person, unless it will substantially harm the person.
B. The guardian may not interfere with established relationships unless necessary to protect the person from substantial harm.

II. The guardian shall make reasonable efforts to maintain the person's established social and support networks during the person's brief absences from the primary residence.
III. When disposing of the person's assets, the guardian may notify family members and friends and give them the opportunity, with court approval, to obtain assets (particularly those with sentimental value).
IV. The guardian shall make reasonable efforts to preserve property designated in the person's will and other estate planning devices executed by the person.

V. The guardian may maintain communication with the person's family and friends regarding significant occurrences that affect the person when that communication would benefit the person.
VI. The guardian may keep immediate family members and friends advised of all pertinent medical issues when doing so would benefit the person. The guardian may request and consider family input when making medical decisions.

Note: Refer to Standard 11 as it relates to confidentiality issues.

NGA Standard 5—The Guardian's Relationship with Other Professionals and Providers of Service to the Person

I. The guardian shall treat all professionals and service providers with courtesy and respect and shall strive to enhance cooperation on behalf of the person.
II. The guardian shall develop and maintain a working knowledge of the services, providers and facilities available in the community.
III. The guardian shall stay current with changes in community resources to ensure that the person under guardianship receives high-quality services from the most appropriate provider.
IV. A guardian who is not a family member guardian may not provide direct service to the person. The guardian shall coordinate and monitor services needed by the person to ensure that the person is receiving the appropriate care and treatment.
V. The guardian shall engage the services of professionals (attorneys, accountants, stock brokers, real estate agents, physicians) as necessary to appropriately meet the goals, needs, and preferences of the person.
VI. The guardian shall make a good faith effort to cooperate with other surrogate decision-makers for the person. These include, where applicable, any other guardian, agent under a power of attorney, health care proxy, trustee, VA fiduciary and representative payee.
VII. The guardian may consider mentoring new guardians.

NGA Standard 6—Informed Consent

I. Decisions the guardian makes on behalf of the person under guardianship shall be based on the principle of Informed Consent.
II. Informed Consent is an individual's agreement to a particular course of action based on a full disclosure of facts needed to make the decision intelligently.
III. Informed Consent is based on adequate information on the issue, voluntary action, and lack of coercion.

IV. The guardian stands in the place of the person and is entitled to the same information and freedom of choice as the person would have received if he or she were not under guardianship.

V. In evaluating each requested decision, the guardian shall do the following:

A. Have a clear understanding of the issue for which informed consent is being sought,
B. Have a clear understanding of the options, expected outcomes, risks and benefits of each alternative,
C. Determine the conditions that necessitate treatment or action,
D. Encourage and support the person in understanding the facts and directing a decision,
E. Maximize the participation of the person in making the decision,
F. Determine whether the person has previously stated preferences in regard to a decision of this nature,
G. Determine why this decision needs to be made now rather than later,
H. Determine what will happen if a decision is made to take no action,
I. Determine what the least restrictive alternative is for the situation,
J. Obtain a second medical or professional opinion, if necessary,
K. Obtain information or input from family and from other professionals, and
L. Obtain written documentation of all reports relevant to each decision.

NGA Standard 7—Standards for Decision-Making

I. Each decision made by the guardian shall be an informed decision based on the principle of Informed Consent as set forth in Standard 6.

II. The guardian shall identify and advocate for the person's goals, needs, and preferences. Goals are what are important to the person under guardianship, whereas preferences are specific expressions of choice.

A. First, the guardian shall ask the person what he or she wants.
B. Second, if the person has difficulty expressing what he or she wants, the guardian shall do everything possible to help the person express his or her goals, needs, and preferences.
C. Third, only when the person, even with assistance, cannot express his or her goals and preferences, shall the guardian seek input from others familiar with the person to determine what the individual would have wanted.
D. Finally, only when the person's goals and preferences cannot be ascertained, may the guardian make a decision in the person's best interest.

III. Substituted Judgment

A. Substituted Judgment is the principle of decision-making that substitutes the decision the person would have made when the person had capacity as the guiding force in any surrogate decision the guardian makes.
B. Substituted Judgment promotes the underlying values of self-determination and well-being of the person.
C. Substituted Judgment is not used when following the person's wishes would cause substantial harm to the person or when the guardian cannot establish the person's goals and preferences even with support.

IV. Best Interest

A. Best Interest is the principle of decision-making that should be used only when the person has never had capacity, when the person's goals and preferences cannot be ascertained even with support, or when following the person's wishes would cause substantial harm to the person.
B. The Best Interest principle requires the guardian to consider the least intrusive, most normalizing, and least restrictive course of action possible to provide for the needs of the person.
C. The Best Interest principle requires the guardian to consider past practice and evaluate reliable evidence of likely choices.

NGA Standard 8—Least Restrictive Alternative

I. The guardian shall carefully evaluate the alternatives that are available and choose the one that best meets the personal and financial goals, needs, and preferences of the person under guardianship while placing the least restrictions on his or her freedom, rights, and ability to control his or her environment.
II. The guardian shall weigh the risks and benefits and develop a balance between maximizing the independence and self-determination of the person and maintaining the person's dignity, protection and safety.
III. The guardian shall make individualized decisions. The least restrictive alternative for one person might not be the least restrictive alternative for another person.
IV. The following guidelines apply in the determination of the least restrictive alternative:

A. The guardian shall become familiar with the available options for residence, care, medical treatment, vocational training, and education.
B. The guardian shall strive to know the person's goals and preferences.

C. The guardian shall consider assessments of the person's needs as determined by specialists. This may include an independent assessment of the person's functional ability, health status, and care needs.

NGA Standard 9—Self-Determination of the Person

I. The guardian shall provide the person under guardianship with every opportunity to exercise those individual rights that the person might be capable of exercising as they relate to the personal care and financial needs of the person.
II. The guardian shall attempt to maximize the self-reliance and independence of the person.
III. The guardian shall encourage the person to participate, to the maximum extent of the person's abilities, in all decisions that affect him or her, to act on his or her own behalf in all matters in which the person is able to do so, and to develop or regain his or her own capacity to the maximum extent possible.
IV. The guardian shall make and implement a plan that seeks to fulfill the person's goals, needs, and preferences. The plan shall emphasize the person's strengths, skills, and abilities to the fullest extent in order to favor the least restrictive setting.
V. The guardian shall wherever possible, seek to ensure that the person leads the planning process; and at a minimum to ensure that the person participates in the process.

NGA Standard 10—The Guardian's Duties Regarding Diversity and Personal Preferences of the Person

I. The guardian shall determine the extent to which the person under guardianship identifies with particular ethnic, religious, and cultural values. To determine these values, the guardian shall also consider the following:

   A. The person's attitudes regarding illness, pain, and suffering,
   B. The person's attitudes regarding death and dying,
   C. The person's views regarding quality of life issues,
   D. The person's views regarding societal roles and relationships, and
   E. The person's attitudes regarding funeral and burial customs.

II. The guardian shall acknowledge the person's right to interpersonal relationships and sexual expression. The guardian shall take steps to ensure that a person's sexual expression is consensual, that the person is not victimized, and that an environment conducive to this expression in privacy is provided.

A. The guardian shall ensure that the person has information about and access to accommodations necessary to permit sexual expression to the extent the person desires and to the extent the person possesses the capacity to consent to the specific activity.
B. The guardian shall take reasonable measures to protect the health and well-being of the person.
C. The guardian shall ensure that the person is informed of birth control methods. The guardian shall consider birth control options and choose the option that provides the person the level of protection appropriate to the person's lifestyle and ability, while considering the preferences of the person. The guardian shall encourage the person, where possible and appropriate, to participate in the choice of a birth control method.
D. The guardian shall protect the rights of the person with regard to sexual expression and preference. A review of ethnic, religious, and cultural values may be necessary to uphold the person's values and customs.

NGA Standard 11—Confidentiality

I. The guardian shall keep the affairs of the person under guardianship confidential.
II. The guardian shall respect the person's privacy and dignity, especially when the disclosure of information is necessary.
III. Disclosure of information shall be limited to what is necessary and relevant to the issue being addressed.
IV. The guardian may disclose or assist the person in communicating sensitive information to the person's family and friends, as defined by the person, unless it will substantially harm the person.
V. The guardian may refuse to disclose sensitive information about the person where disclosure would be detrimental to the well-being of the person or would subject the person's estate to undue risk. Such a refusal to disclose information must be reported to the court.

NGA Standard 12—Duties of the Guardian of the Person

I. The guardian shall have the following duties and obligations to the person under guardianship unless the order of appointment provides otherwise:

A. To see that the person is living in the most appropriate environment that addresses the person's goals, needs, and preferences.
1. The guardian shall have a strong priority for home or other community-based settings, when not inconsistent with the person's goals and preferences.

2. The guardian shall authorize moving a person to a more restrictive environment only after evaluating other medical and health care options and making an independent determination that the move is the least restrictive alternative at the time, fulfills the current needs of the person and serves the overall best interest of the person.
3. The guardian shall consider the proximity of the setting to those people and activities that are important to the person when choosing a residential setting.
4. At a minimum the guardian shall report to a court before a move to a more restrictive residential setting, and the justification for the move.
5. When the guardian considers involuntary or long-term placement of the person in an institutional setting, the bases of the decision shall be to minimize the risk of substantial harm to the person, to obtain the most appropriate placement possible, and to secure the best treatment for the person.

B. To ensure that provision is made for the support, care, comfort, health, and maintenance of the person.

C. To make reasonable efforts to secure for the person medical, psychological, therapeutic, and social services, training, education, and social and vocational opportunities that are appropriate and that will maximize the person's potential for self-reliance and independence.

D. To keep the affairs of the person confidential, except when it is necessary to disclose such affairs for the best interests of the person.

E. To seek specific judicial authority when a civil commitment, the dissolution of a marriage, or another extraordinary circumstance is being addressed.

F. To file with the court, on a timely basis but not less often than annually, all reports required by state statute, regulations, court rule, or the particular court pursuant to whose authority the guardian was appointed.

G. To adhere to the requirements of Standard 17—Duties of the Guardian of the Estate and Standard 18—Guardian of the Estate: Initial and Ongoing Responsibilities, to the extent that the guardian of the person has been authorized by the court to manage the person's property.

H. To petition the court for limitation or termination of the guardianship when the person no longer meets the standard pursuant to which the guardianship was imposed, or when there is an effective alternative available.

I. To promptly report to the appropriate authorities any abuse, neglect and/or exploitation as defined by state statutes.

NGA Standard 13—Guardian of the Person: Initial and Ongoing Responsibilities

I. With the proper authority, initial steps after appointment as guardian are as follows:

A. The guardian shall address all issues of the person under guardianship that require immediate action.
B. The guardian shall meet with the person as soon after the appointment as is feasible. At the first meeting, the guardian shall:

1. Communicate to the person the role of the guardian;
2. Explain the rights retained by the person;
3. Assess the person's physical and social situation, the person's educational, vocational, and recreational needs, the person's preferences, and the support systems available to the person; and

C. Attempt to gather any missing necessary information regarding the person.

II. After the first meeting with the person, the guardian shall notify relevant agencies and individuals of the appointment of a guardian and shall complete the intake process by gathering information and ensuring that certain evaluations are completed, if appropriate. The guardian shall:

A. Obtain an evaluation of the person's condition, treatment, and functional status from the person's treating physician or appropriate specialist, if a comprehensive medical evaluation was not completed as part of the petitioning process, or has not been done within the past year.

1. Obtain a psychological evaluation, if appropriate.
2. Obtain an inventory of advance directives. Such statements of intent would include, but are not limited to, powers of attorney, living wills, organ donation statements and statements by the person recorded in medical charts.

B. Establish contact with and develop a regular pattern of communication with the guardian of the estate or any other fiduciary for the person.

III. The guardian shall develop and implement a written guardianship plan setting forth short-term and long-term objectives for meeting the goals, needs and preferences of the person.

A. The plan shall emphasize a "person-centered philosophy."
B. The plan must address medical, psychiatric, social, vocational, educational, training, residential, and recreational goals, needs and preferences of the person.
C. The plan must also address whether the person's finances and budget are in line with the services the person needs and are flexible enough to deal with the changing status of the person.

D. Short-term goals must reflect the first year of guardianship, and long-term goals must reflect the time after the first year.
E. The plan must be based on a multidisciplinary functional assessment.
F. The plan must be updated no less often than annually.

IV. The guardian shall maintain a separate file for each person. The file must include, at a minimum, the following information and documents:

A. The person's name, date of birth, address, telephone number, Social Security number, medical coverage, physician, diagnoses, medications, and allergies to medications;
B. All legal documents involving the person;
C. Advance directives;
D. A list of key contacts;
E. A list of service providers, contact information, a description of services provided to the person, and progress/status reports;
F. A list of all over-the-counter and prescribed medication the person is taking, the dosage, the reason why it is taken, and the name of the doctor prescribing the medication;
G. Documentation of all client and collateral contacts, including the date, time, and activity;
H. Progress notes that are as detailed as necessary to reflect contacts made and work done regarding the person;
I. The guardianship plan;
J. An inventory, if required;
K. Assessments regarding the person's past and present medical, psychological, and social functioning;
L. Documentation of the person's known values, lifestyle preferences, and known wishes regarding medical and other care and service; and
M. A photograph of the person.

V. The guardian shall visit the person no less than monthly.

A. The guardian shall assess the person's physical appearance and condition and assess the appropriateness of the person's current living situation and the continuation of existing services, taking into consideration all aspects of social, psychological, educational, direct services, and health and personal care needs as well as the need for any additional services.
B. The guardian shall maintain substantive communication with service providers, caregivers, and others attending to the person.
C. The guardian shall participate in all care or planning conferences concerning the residential, educational, vocational, or rehabilitation program of the person.
D. The guardian shall require that each service provider develop an appropriate service plan for the person and shall take appropriate action to ensure that the service plans are being implemented.

E. The guardian shall regularly examine all services and all charts, notes, logs, evaluations, and other documents regarding the person at the place of residence and at any program site to ascertain that the care plan is being properly followed.

F. The guardian shall advocate on behalf of the person with staff in an institutional setting and other residential placements. The guardian shall assess the overall quality of services provided to the person, using accepted regulations and care standards as guidelines and seeking remedies when care is found to be deficient.

G. The guardian shall monitor the residential setting on an ongoing basis and take any necessary action when the setting does not meet the individual's current goals, needs and preferences, including but not limited to:

1. Evaluating the plan;
2. Enforcing residents' rights, legal and civil rights; and
3. Ensuring quality of care and appropriateness of the setting in light of the feelings and attitudes of the person.

VI. The guardian shall fully identify, examine, and continue to seek information regarding options that will fulfill the person's goals, needs, and preferences.

A. Guardians shall take full advantage of professional assistance in identifying all available options for long term services and supports.

B. Sources of professional assistance include but are not limited to area agencies on aging, centers for independent living, protection and advocacy agencies, long-term care ombudsmen, developmental disabilities councils, aging and disability resource centers, and community mental health agencies.

VII. The guardian shall obtain and maintain a current understanding of what is required and expected of the guardian, statutory and local court rule requirements, and necessary filings and reports.

VIII. The guardian shall become educated about the nature of any incapacity, condition and functional capabilities of the person.

NGA Standard 14—Decision-Making About Medical Treatment

I. The guardian shall promote, monitor, and maintain the health and well-being of the person under guardianship.

II. The guardian shall ensure that all medical care for the person is appropriately provided and that the person is treated with dignity.

III. The guardian shall seek to ensure that the person receives appropriate health care consistent with person-centered health care decision-making.

IV. The guardian, in making health care decisions or seeking court approval for a decision, shall:

A. Maximize the participation of the person,
B. Acquire a clear understanding of the medical facts,
C. Acquire a clear understanding of the health care options and the risks and benefits of each option, and
D. Encourage and support the individual in understanding the facts and directing a decision.

V. Use the substituted judgment standard with respect to a health care decision unless the guardian cannot determine person's prior wishes.

VI. The guardian shall determine whether the person, before the appointment of a guardian, executed any advance directives, such as powers of attorney, living wills, organ donation statements and statements by the person recorded in medical charts. On finding such documents, the guardian shall inform the court and other interested parties of the existing health care documents.

VII. To the extent the person cannot currently direct the decision, the guardian shall act in accordance with the person's prior general statements, actions, values, and preferences to the extent actually known or ascertainable by the guardian.

VIII. If the person's preferences are unknown and unascertainable, the guardian shall act in accordance with reasonable information received from professionals and persons who demonstrate sufficient interest in the person's welfare, to determine the person's best interests, which determination shall include consideration of consequences for others that an individual in the person's circumstances would consider.

IX. Absent an emergency or the person's execution of a living will, durable power of attorney for health care, or other advance directive declaration of intent that clearly indicates the person's wishes with respect to a medical intervention, a guardian who has authority may not grant or deny authorization for a medical intervention until he or she has given careful consideration to the criteria listed in Standards 6 and 7.

X. In the event of an emergency, a guardian who has authority to make health care decisions shall grant or deny authorization of emergency medical treatment based on a reasonable assessment of the criteria listed in Standards 6 and 7, within the time allotted by the emergency.

XI. The guardian shall seek a second opinion for any medical treatment or intervention that would cause a reasonable person to do so or in circumstances where any medical intervention poses a significant risk to the person. The guardian shall obtain a second opinion from an independent physician.

XII. Under extraordinary medical circumstances, in addition to assessing the criteria and using the resources outlined in Standards 6 and 7, the guardian shall enlist ethical, legal, and medical advice, with particular attention to the advice of ethics committees in hospitals and elsewhere.

XIII. The guardian shall speak directly with the treating or attending physician before authorizing or denying any medical treatment.

XIV. The guardian may not authorize extraordinary procedures without prior authorization from the court unless the person has executed a living will or durable power of attorney that clearly indicates the person's desire with respect to that action. Extraordinary procedures may include, but are not limited to, the following medical interventions:

A. Psychosurgery,
B. Experimental treatment,
C. Sterilization,
D. Abortion, and
E. Electroshock therapy.

XV. The guardian shall seek to ensure that appropriate palliative care is incorporated into all health care, unless not in accordance with the person's preferences and values.

XVI. The guardian shall keep individuals that are important to the person reasonably informed of important health care decisions.

NGA Standard 15—Decision-Making About Withholding and Withdrawal of Medical Treatment

I. The NGA recognizes that there are circumstances in which, with the approval of the court if necessary, it is legally and ethically justifiable to consent to the withholding or withdrawal of medical treatment, including artificially provided nutrition and hydration, on behalf of the person under guardianship. In making this determination there shall in all cases be a presumption in favor of the continued treatment of the person.

II. If the person had expressed or currently expresses a preference regarding the withholding or withdrawal of medical treatment, the guardian shall follow the wishes of the person. If the person's current wishes are in conflict with wishes previously expressed when the person had capacity, the guardian shall have this ethical dilemma reviewed by an ethics committee and if necessary, submit the issue to the court for direction.

III. When making this decision on behalf of the person, the guardian shall gather and document information as outlined in Standard 6 and shall follow Standard 7.

NGA Standard 16—Conflict of Interest: Ancillary and Support Services

I. The guardian shall avoid all conflicts of interest and self-dealing or the appearance of a conflict of interest and self-dealing when addressing the needs of the person under guardianship. Impropriety or conflict of interest arises where the guardian has some personal or agency interest that can be perceived as self-serving or adverse to the position or best interest of the person. Self-dealing arises when the guardian seeks to take advantage of his or her position as a guardian and acts for his or her own interests rather than for the interests of the person.

II. The guardian shall become fully educated as to what constitutes a conflict of interest and self-dealing, and why they should be avoided.

III. Rules relating to specific ancillary and support service situations that might create an impropriety or conflict of interest include the following:

A. The guardian may not directly provide housing, medical, legal, or other direct services to the person. Some direct services may be approved by the court for family guardians.

1. The guardian shall coordinate and assure the provision of all necessary services to the person rather than providing those services directly.

2. The guardian shall be independent from all service providers, thus ensuring that the guardian remains free to challenge inappropriate or poorly delivered services and to advocate on behalf of the person.

3. When a guardian can demonstrate unique circumstances indicating that no other entity is available to act as guardian, or to provide needed direct services, an exception can be made, provided that the exception is in the best interest of the person. Reasons for the exception must be documented and the court notified.

B. A guardianship program must be a freestanding entity and must not be subject to undue influence.

C. When a guardianship program is a part of a larger organization or governmental entity, there must be an arm's-length relationship with the larger organization or governmental entity and it shall have independent decision-making ability.

D. The guardian may not be in a position of representing both the person and the service provider.

E. A guardian who is not a family guardian may act as petitioner only when no other entity is available to act, provided all alternatives have been exhausted.

F. The guardian shall consider all possible consequences of serving the dual roles of guardian and expert witness. Serving in both roles may present a conflict. The guardian's primary duty and responsibility is always to the person.

G. The guardian may not employ his or her friends or family to provide services for a profit or fee unless no alternative is available and the guardian discloses this arrangement to the court.

H. The guardian shall neither solicit nor accept incentives from service providers.
I. The guardian shall consider various ancillaries or support service providers and select the providers that best meet the needs of the person.
J. A guardian who is an attorney or employs attorneys may provide legal services to a person only when doing so best meets the needs of the person and is approved by the court following full disclosure of the conflict of interest. The guardian who is an attorney shall ensure that the services and fees are differentiated and are reasonable. The services and fees are subject to court approval.
K. The guardian may enter into a transaction that may be a conflict of interest only when necessary, or when there is a significant benefit to the person under the guardianship, and shall disclose such transactions to interested parties and obtain prior court approval.

NGA Standard 17—Duties of the Guardian of the Estate

I. The guardian, as a fiduciary, shall manage the financial affairs of the person under guardianship in a way that maximizes the dignity, autonomy, and self-determination of the person.
II. When making decisions the guardian shall:
   A. Give priority to the goals, needs and preferences of the person, and
   B. Weigh the costs and benefits to the estate.
III. The guardian shall consider the current wishes, past practices, and reliable evidence of likely choices. If substantial harm would result or there is no reliable evidence of likely choices, the guardian shall consider the best interests of the person.
IV. The guardian shall assist and encourage the person to act on his or her own behalf and to participate in decisions.
V. The guardian shall use reasonable efforts to provide oversight to any income and assets under the control of the person.
VI. The guardian shall, consistent with court order and state statutes, exercise authority only as necessitated by the limitations of the person.
VII. The guardian shall act in a manner above reproach, and his or her actions will be open to scrutiny at all times.
VIII. The guardian shall provide competent management of the person's property and, shall supervise all income and disbursements of the estate.
IX. The guardian shall manage the estate only for the benefit of the person.
X. The guardian shall keep estate assets safe by keeping accurate records of all transactions and be able to fully account for all the assets in the estate.
XI. The guardian shall keep estate money separate from the guardian's personal money; the guardian shall keep the money of individual estates

separate unless accurate separate accounting exists within the combined accounts.

XII. The guardian shall make claims against others on behalf of the estate as deemed in the best interest of the person and shall defend against actions that would result in a loss of estate assets.

XIII. The guardian shall apply state law regarding prudent investment practices, including seeking responsible consultation with and delegation to people with appropriate expertise when managing the estate.

XIV. The guardian shall employ prudent accounting procedures when managing the estate.

XV. The guardian shall determine if a will exists and obtain a copy to determine how to manage estate assets and property.

XVI. The guardian shall obtain and maintain a current understanding of what is required and expected of the guardian, statutory and local court rule requirements, and necessary filings and reports.

XVII. The guardian shall promptly report to the appropriate authorities abuse, neglect and/or exploitation as defined by state statute.

NGA Standard 18—Guardian of the Estate: Initial and Ongoing Responsibilities

I. With the proper authority, the initial steps after appointment as guardian are as follows:

   A. The guardian shall address all issues of the estate that require immediate action, which include, but are not limited to, securing all real and personal property, insuring it at current market value, and taking the steps necessary to protect it from damage, destruction, or loss.

      1. The guardian shall ascertain the income, assets, and liabilities of the person.
      2. The guardian shall ascertain the goals, needs and preferences of the person.
      3. The guardian shall coordinate and consult with others close to the person.

   B. The guardian shall meet with the person under guardianship as soon after the appointment as feasible. At the first meeting the guardian shall:

      1. Communicate to the person the role of the guardian;
      2. Outline the rights retained by the person and the grievance procedures available;
      3. Assess the previously and currently expressed wishes of the person and evaluate them based on current acuity; and
      4. Attempt to gather from the person any necessary information regarding the estate.

II. The guardian shall become educated about the nature of any incapacity, condition and functional capabilities of the person.

III. The guardian shall develop and implement a financial plan and budget for the management of income and assets that corresponds with the care plan for the person and aims to address the goals, needs and preferences of the person. The guardian of the estate and the guardian of the person (if one exists) or other health care decision-maker shall communicate regularly and coordinate efforts with regard to the care and financial plans, as well as other events that might affect the person.

   A. Guardian shall value the well-being of the person over the preservation of the estate.
   B. Guardian shall maintain the goal of managing, but not necessarily eliminating, risks.
   C. The financial plan shall emphasize a "person-centered philosophy."

IV. The guardian shall take all steps necessary to obtain a bond to protect the estate, including obtaining a court order.

V. The guardian shall obtain all public and insurance benefits for which the person is eligible.

VI. The guardian shall thoroughly document the management of the estate and the carrying out of any and all duties required by statute or regulation.

VII. The guardian shall prepare an inventory of all property for which he or she is responsible. The inventory must list all the assets owned by the person with their values on the date the guardian was appointed and must be independently verified.

VIII. All accountings must contain sufficient information to clearly describe all significant transactions affecting administration during the accounting period. All accountings must be complete, accurate, and understandable.

IX. The guardian shall oversee the disposition of the person's assets to qualify the person for any public benefits program.

X. On the termination of the guardianship or the death of the person, the guardian shall facilitate the appropriate closing of the estate and submit a final accounting to the court.

XI. The guardian may monitor, provide oversight or manage the personal allowance of the person.

XII. The guardian shall, when appropriate, open a burial trust account and make funeral arrangements for the person.

NGA Standard 19—Property Management

I. The guardian may not dispose of real or personal property of the person under guardianship without judicial, administrative, or other independent review.

II. In the absence of reliable evidence of the person's views before the appointment of a guardian, the guardian, having the proper authority, may not sell, encumber, convey, or otherwise transfer property of the person, or an interest in that property, unless doing so is in the best interest of the person.

III. In considering whether to dispose of the person's property, the guardian shall consider the following:

   A. Whether disposing of the property will benefit or improve the life of the person,
   B. The likelihood that the person will need or benefit from the property in the future,
   C. The previously expressed or current desires of the person with regard to the property,
   D. The provisions of the person's estate plan as it relates to the property, if any,
   E. The tax consequences of the transaction,
   F. The impact of the transaction on the person's entitlement to public benefits,
   G. The condition of the entire estate,
   H. The ability of the person to maintain the property,
   I. The availability and appropriateness of alternatives to the disposition of the property,
   J. The likelihood that property may deteriorate or be subject to waste, and
   K. The benefits versus the liability and costs of maintaining the property.

IV. The guardian shall consider the necessity for an independent appraisal of real and personal property.

V. The guardian shall provide for insurance coverage, as appropriate, for property in the estate.

NGA Standard 20—Conflict of Interest: Estate, Financial, and Business Services

I. The guardian shall avoid all conflicts of interest and self-dealing or the appearance of a conflict of interest and self-dealing when addressing the needs of the person under guardianship. Impropriety or conflict of interest arises where the guardian has some personal or agency interest that can be perceived as self-serving or adverse to the position or best interest of the person. Self-dealing arises when the guardian seeks to take advantage of his or her position as a guardian and acts for his or her own interests rather than for the interests of the person.

II. Rules relating to specific situations that might create an impropriety or conflict of interest include the following:

A. The guardian may not commingle personal or program funds with the funds of the person, except as follows:
   1. This standard does not prohibit the guardian from consolidating and maintaining a person's funds in joint accounts with the funds of other persons.
   2. If the guardian maintains joint accounts, separate and complete accounting of each person's funds shall also be maintained by the guardian.
   3. When an individual or organization serves several persons, it may be more efficient and more cost-effective to pool the individual estate funds in a single account. In this manner, banking fees and costs are distributed, rather than being borne by each estate separately.
   4. If the court allows the use of combined accounts, they should be permitted only where the guardian has available resources to keep accurate records of the exact amount of funds in the account, including allocation of interest and charges attributable to each estate based on the asset level of the person.

B. The guardian may not sell, encumber, convey, or otherwise transfer the person's real or personal property or any interest in that property to himself or herself, a spouse, a coworker, an employee, a member of the board of the agency or corporate guardian, an agent, or an attorney, or any corporation or trust in which the guardian has a substantial beneficial interest.

C. The guardian may not sell or otherwise convey to the person property from any of the parties noted above.

D. The guardian may not loan or give money or objects of worth from the person's estate unless specific prior approval is obtained.

E. The guardian may not use the person's income and assets to support or benefit other individuals directly or indirectly unless specific prior approval is obtained and a reasonable showing is made that such support is consistent with the person's goals, needs and preferences and will not substantially harm the estate.

F. The guardian may not borrow funds from, or lend funds to, the person unless there is prior notice of the proposed transaction to interested persons and others as directed by the court or agency administering the person's benefits, and the transaction is approved by the court.

G. The guardian may not profit from any transactions made on behalf of the person's estate at the expense of the estate, nor may the guardian compete with the estate, unless prior approval is obtained from the court.

NGA Standard 21—Termination and Limitation of Guardianship

I. Limited guardianship of the person and estate is preferred over a plenary guardianship.
II. The guardian shall assist the person under guardianship to develop or regain the capacity to manage his or her personal and financial affairs.
III. The guardian shall seek termination or limitation of the guardianship in the following circumstances:

   A. When the person has developed or regained capacity in areas in which he or she was found incapacitated by the court,
   B. When less restrictive alternatives exist,
   C. When the person expresses the desire to challenge the necessity of all or part of the guardianship,
   D. When the person has died, or
   E. When the guardianship no longer benefits the person.

NGA Standard 22—Guardianship Service Fees

I. Guardians are entitled to reasonable compensation for their services.
II. The guardian shall bear in mind at all times the responsibility to conserve the person's estate when making decisions regarding providing guardianship services and charging a fee for those services.
III. All fees related to the duties of the guardianship must be reviewed and approved by the court. Fees must be reasonable and be related only to guardianship duties.
IV. The guardian shall:

   A. Disclose in writing the basis for fee (e.g., rate schedule) at the time of the guardian's first appearance in the action,
   B. Disclose a projection of annual fiduciary fees within 90 days of appointment,
   C. Disclose fee changes,
   D. Seek authorization for fee-generating actions not contained in the fiduciary's appointment, and
   E. Disclose a detailed explanation for any claim for fiduciary fees.

V. A guardian shall report to the court any likelihood that funds will be exhausted and advise the court whether the guardian intends to seek removal when there are no longer funds to pay fees. A guardian may not abandon the person when estate funds are exhausted and shall make appropriate succession plans.
VI. A guardian may seek payment of fiduciary fees from the income of a person receiving Medicaid services only after the deduction of the

personal needs allowance, spousal allowance and health care insurance premiums.

VII. Factors to be considered in determining reasonableness of the guardian's fees include:

A. Powers and responsibilities under the court appointment;
B. Necessity of the services;
C. The request for compensation in comparison to a previously disclosed basis for fees, and the amount authorized in the approved budget, including any legal presumption of reasonableness or necessity;
D. The guardian's expertise, training, education, experience, professional standing, and skill, including whether an appointment in a particular matter precluded other employment;
E. The character of the work to be done, including difficulty, intricacy, importance, time, skill, or license required, or responsibility undertaken;
F. The conditions or circumstances of the work, including emergency matters requiring urgent attention, services provided outside of regular business hours, potential danger (e.g., hazardous materials, contaminated real property, or dangerous persons), or other extraordinary conditions;
G. The work actually performed, including the time actually expended, and the attention and skill-level required for each task, including whether a different person could have rendered the service better, cheaper, faster;
H. The result, specifically whether the guardian was successful, what benefits to the person were derived from the efforts, and whether probable benefits exceeded costs;
I. Whether the guardian timely disclosed that a projected cost was likely to exceed the probable benefit, affording the court the opportunity to modify its order in furtherance of the best interest of the estate;
J. The fees customarily paid, and time customarily expended, for performing like services in the community, including whether the court has previously approved similar fees in another comparable matter;
K. The degree of financial or professional risk and responsibility assumed;
L. The fidelity and loyalty displayed by the guardian, including whether the guardian put the best interests of the estate before the economic interest of the guardian to continue the engagement; and
M. The need for a local availability of specialized knowledge and the need for retaining outside fiduciaries to avoid conflict of interest.

VIII. Fees or expenses charged by the guardian shall be documented through billings maintained by the guardian. If time records are maintained, they shall clearly and accurately state:

A. Date and time spent on a task,
B. Duty performed,
C. Expenses incurred,
D. Collateral contacts involved, and
E. Identification of individual who performed the duty (e.g., guardian, staff, volunteer).

IX. All parties should respect the privacy and dignity of the person when disclosing information regarding fees.

NGA Standard 23—Management of Multiple Guardianship Cases

I. The guardian shall limit each caseload to a size that allows the guardian to accurately and adequately support and protect the person, that allows a minimum of one visit per month with each person, and that allows regular contact with all service providers.
II. The size of any caseload must be based on an objective evaluation of the activities expected, the time that may be involved in each case, other demands made on the guardian, and ancillary support available to the guardian.

A. The guardian may institute a system to evaluate the level of difficulty of each guardianship case to which the guardian is assigned or appointed.
B. The outcome of the evaluation must clearly indicate the complexity of the decisions to be made, the complexity of the estate to be managed, and the time spent. The guardian shall use the evaluation as a guide for determining how many cases the individual guardian may manage.

NGA Standard 24—Quality Assurance

I. Guardians shall actively pursue and facilitate periodic independent review of their provision of guardianship services.
II. The independent review shall occur periodically, but no less often than every two years, and must include a review of a representative sample of cases.
III. The independent review must include, but is not limited to, a review of agency policies and procedures, a review of records, and a visit with the person and with the individual providing direct service to the person.
IV. An independent review may be obtained from:

A. A court monitoring system,
B. An independent peer, or
C. An CGC national master guardian.

V. The quality assurance review does not replace other monitoring requirements established by the court.

NGA Standard 25—Sale or Purchase of a Guardianship Practice

I. Guardianship is a fiduciary relationship and as such is bound by the fiduciary obligations recognized by the community and the law.

II. A guardianship practice is defined as private, professional guardianship services provided to two or more individuals found by a court to be incapacitated and in need of a guardian.

III. A professional guardian may choose to sell all or substantially all of a guardianship practice, including goodwill, subject to the following guidelines:

   A. A professional guardian considering the sale of a guardianship practice shall ensure that the persons are considered in the sale process and that guardianship responsibilities continue to be met during the transition.

   B. The professional guardian shall require documentation of the purchaser's references pertaining to qualifications to serve as guardian, as defined by state statutes.

   C. Sale of a guardianship practice to a purchaser engaged in serving or representing any interest adverse to the interest of the persons is not appropriate.

   D. The sale price for the guardianship practice must not be the sole consideration in selecting the purchaser.

   E. The professional guardian shall provide formal written notice of the proposed sale to the court, to the persons, and to other interested parties, even if not required by state statutes.

   F. Consideration should be given to requesting that the court appoint a guardian ad litem, or another third party reviewer, to protect the interests of the persons.

   G. All parties to the sale of the guardianship practice shall take steps to ensure the continuity of care and protection for the persons during the period of the sale and transfer of ownership.

   H. The professional guardian may not disclose confidential information regarding a person for the purpose of inducing a sale of a guardianship practice.

   I. The fees charged to existing persons may not be increased by the purchaser of a guardianship practice solely for the purpose of financing the purchase.

IV. Admission to, employment by, or retirement from a guardianship practice, retirement plans or similar arrangements, or sale of tangible assets of a guardianship practice may not be considered a sale or purchase under this standard.

NGA and CGC Qualifications for Court-Appointed Guardians

Corporate Guardian—A corporate guardian is a corporation that is named as guardian for an individual and may receive compensation in its role as guardian with court approval. Corporate guardians may include banks, trust departments, for-profit entities, and nonprofit entities. A corporate guardian:

1. Shall follow the *NGA Ethical Principles.*
2. Shall follow the *NGA Standards of Practice.*
3. Should strive to have decision-making staff become national certified guardians and national master guardians.

Family Guardian—A family guardian is an individual who is appointed as guardian for a person to whom he or she is related by blood or marriage. In most cases when there is a willing and able family member who has no conflict with the prospective person, the court prefers to appoint the family member as guardian. On court approval, a family guardian may receive reasonable compensation for time and expenses relating to care of the person. A family guardian:

1. Is encouraged to recognize the resources available through the NGA.
2. Shall follow the *NGA Ethical Principles.*
3. Shall follow the *NGA Standards of Practice* when carrying out guardianship responsibilities.

Individual Professional Guardian—An individual professional guardian is an individual who is not related to the person by blood or marriage and with court approval may receive compensation in his or her role as guardian. He or she usually acts as guardian for two or more individuals. An individual professional guardian:

1. Shall follow the *NGA Ethical Principles.*
2. Shall follow the *NGA Standards of Practice.*
3. Should strive to become a national certified guardian and national master guardian, if applicable.

National Master Guardian—A national master guardian is an individual who has met the qualifications established by the Center for Guardianship Certification. A national master guardian:

1. Shall meet the Master guardian qualifications as established by the Center for Guardianship Certification.
2. Shall follow the *NGA Ethical Principles.*
3. Shall follow the *NGA Standards of Practice.*

Public Guardian—A public guardian is a governmental entity that is named as guardian of an individual and may receive compensation in its role as guardian with court approval. Public guardians may include branches of state, county, or local government. A public guardian:

1. Shall follow the *NGA Ethical Principles.*
2. Shall follow the *NGA Standards of Practice.*
3. Should strive to have decision-making staff become national certified guardians and national master guardians.

National Certified Guardian—A national certified guardian is an individual who has met the qualifications established by the Center for Guardianship Certification. A national certified guardian:

1. Shall meet the National certified guardian qualifications as established by the Center for Guardianship Certification.
2. Shall follow the *NGA Ethical Principles.*
3. Shall follow the *NGA Standards of Practice.*
4. Should strive to become a national master guardian.

Volunteer Guardian—A volunteer guardian is a person who is not related to the person by blood or marriage and who does not receive any compensation in his or her role as guardian. The guardian may receive reimbursement of expenses or a minimum stipend with court approval. A volunteer guardian:

1. Shall follow the *NGA Ethical Principles.*
2. Shall follow the *NGA Standards of Practice.*
3. Is encouraged to become a national certified guardian and national master guardian, if applicable.

APPENDIX C

National Guardianship Association Standards of Practice Checklist

This checklist is designed to allow you to perform a self-audit of your compliance with following the NGA Standards of Practice. It is important that you be able to validate your adherence to these Standards.

Disclaimer

This National Guardianship Association (NGA) Standards of Practice Checklist is designed to assist you with monitoring and improving your application of the NGA Standards of Practice. NGA is committed to promoting excellence in guardianship and we challenge you to practice guardianship at a level higher than the minimum standards often found in state laws.

The checklist is a tool designed to supplement the NGA Standards of Practice. You should fully acquaint yourself with the complete Standards of Practice, available at the NGA website: www.guardianship.org. When completing the checklist, you should refer to the standards of practice to determine if you are in compliance. The completion of this checklist should not lead to any assumption that you are in compliance with the standards of practice or local law. It is your responsibility to continually review your practice and to review the requirements of state law, local law and the standards of practice to continually improve upon your practice of guardianship and to serve your clients in the best manner possible.

Specific state statutes and requirements are not addressed in this checklist. It is the obligation of each individual to know and follow his or her state and local law.

NGA Standard 1—Applicable Law and General Standards

___Yes ___No ___N/A Is the guardian in compliance with the requirements of the court order and applicable law?

NGA Standard 2—The Guardian's Relationship to the Court

___Yes ___No ___N/A Has the guardian/organization established a policy regarding how and when to obtain a court authorization for all actions as required by law or not specified in the court order?

___Yes ___No ___N/A Has the court approved the guardian's fees?

___Yes ___No ___N/A Does the guardian submit reports regarding the status of the guardianship as required by the court or at least annually?

NGA Standard 3—The Guardian's Professional Relationship with the Person

___Yes ___No ___N/A Has the guardian avoided personal relationships with the person, the person's family, or the person's friends?

___Yes ___No If No, did these relationships exist prior to the existence of the guardianship?

___Yes ___No ___N/A Does the guardian engage in sexual relations with the person?

___Yes ___No If Yes, is the person the spouse of the guardian or in a relationship that existed prior to the guardianship?

___Yes ___No ___N/A Is the guardian participating in continuing guardianship education?

NGA Standard 4—The Guardian's Relationship with Family Members and Friends of the Person

___Yes ___No ___N/A Does the guardian encourage and support the person in maintaining contact with family members and friends, as defined by the person?

___Yes ___No ___N/A Does the guardian make reasonable efforts to preserve property designated in the person's will and other estate planning devices executed by the person?

___Yes ___No ___N/A Does the guardian keep immediate family members and friends advised of pertinent medical/financial/placement issues, when doing so benefits the person?

___Yes ___No ___N/A Does the guardian request and consider family input when making medical or financial or placement decisions?

NGA Standard 5—The Guardian's Relationship with Other Professionals and Providers of Service to the Person

___Yes ___No ___N/A Does the guardian maintain a professional approach when working with all other individuals for the benefit of the person?

___Yes ___No ___N/A Has the guardian developed and maintained a working knowledge of services, providers, and facilities available in the community?

___Yes ___No ___N/A Has the guardian stayed current with changes in community resources to ensure that the person received high-quality services from the most appropriate provider?

___Yes ___No ___N/A Does the guardian provide direct services to the person?

___Yes ___No If Yes, is the guardian a family member?

___Yes ___No If Yes, and if compensated, has the guardian secured court approval for compensation?

___Yes ___No ___N/A Does the guardian coordinate and monitor services needed by the person to ensure that the person is receiving the appropriate care and treatment?

___Yes ___No ___N/A Does the guardian engage the services of professionals (attorneys, accountants, stockbrokers, real estate agents, doctors, for example) as necessary to appropriately meet the needs of the person?

NGA Standard 6—Informed Consent

___Yes ___No ___N/A Have the guidelines for making a decision (Informed Consent) been followed?

___Yes ___No ___N/A Was decision(s) made based on adequate information on the issue, a voluntarily action and lack of coercion?

___Yes ___No ___N/A Was there any outside influence placed upon guardian for a particular outcome?

NGA Standard 7—Standards for Decision-Making

___Yes ___No ___N/A Did the decision(s) follow guidelines for Substituted Judgment?

OR

___Yes ___No ___N/A If Substituted Judgment could not be followed, were there efforts to obtain information from others familiar with the person to determine any known preferences?

___Yes ___No ___N/A Did the decision(s) follow guidelines for Best Interests?

NGA Standard 8—Least Restrictive Alternative

___Yes ___No ___N/A Was the outcome(s) of personal freedom, civil rights, placement and environment considered in relationship to striving toward obtaining the least restrictive alternative?

___Yes ___No ___N/A Was there documented evidence to demonstrate the guardian weighed the risks and benefits to develop a balance between maximizing independence, self-determination and maintaining the person's dignity, protection and safety?

___Yes ___No ___N/A Was the least restrictive alternative in placement, health treatment and care available?

___Yes ___No If so, was the least restrictive alternative utilized? If not, justify deviation from the less restrictive alternative.

NGA Standard 9—Self-Determination of the Person

___Yes ___No ___N/A Were the wishes of the person considered in the data collection process in regard to diversity and personal preference?

___Yes ___No ___N/A Is there a person-centered plan developed and implemented to fulfill the person's goals, needs, and preference in order to emphasize the person's strengths, skills and abilities to favor the least restrictive setting? If not, justify deviation from person-centered plan.

___Yes ___ No ___ N/A Did the person for whom the plan was developed participate in the person-centered plan? If not, justify reason for non-participation.

NGA Standard 10—The Guardian's Duties Regarding Diversity and Personal Preferences of the Person

___Yes ___No ___N/A Is there case documentation to demonstrate the guardian identified the particular ethnic, religious, and cultural values of the person under guardianship as described under this Standard?

__Yes __No __N/A Is there case documentation to demonstrate that the guardian has discussed and acknowledged the person's right to interpersonal relationships and sexual expression is consensual?

NGA Standard 11—Confidentiality

__Yes __No __N/A Did anyone gain access to information about the person who does not directly provide support to him or her?

__Yes __No __N/A Was information shared when appropriate with family, friends, and other social contacts to assure that the person maintains these contacts?

NGA Standard 12—Duties of the Guardian of the Person

Assure the person is living in the most appropriate environment:

__Yes __No __N/A By assuring the person's wishes (geography, transportation, support from family, friends, spiritual advisers, etc.) ascertained?

__Yes __ No If ascertained, were the person's wishes followed? If not, justify why.

__Yes __No __N/A By assuring the person's needs (work, school, medical care, shopping etc.) are assessed, and fulfilled when appropriate?

Are provisions in place for:

__Yes __No __N/A End of life provisions (funeral, burial, disposition of assets)

__Yes __No __N/A Care, comfort and support (opportunities for mental stimulation, nutrition, personal hygiene, exercise/therapy, socialization/recreation/vocational/religious activities, asset safeguards)

__Yes __No __N/A Health and safety (mental/dental needs addressed, safe and nurturing environment, personal needs fulfilled; environmental reviews of potential safety hazards)

__Yes __No __N/A Medical reviews and treatment evaluation (regularly scheduled physical/psychological checkups; mediation review)

___Yes ___No ___N/A Maintaining confidentiality (written policies/procedures and guardian orientations)

___Yes ___No ___N/A Procedures for conditions/situations under which specific judicial approval must be sought:

___Yes ___No ___N/A Is the person's living situation in the least restrictive setting unless the person understands his/her choices and chooses a more restrictive environment?

___Yes ___No ___N/A Does the person's residential location maximize his/her potential contact with friends, family and other social contacts?

___Yes ___No ___N/A Procedures and due date schedules for court filings/reporting's (on a timely basis but not less often than annually)

___Yes ___No ___N/A Adherence to Standard 17 (Duties of the Guardian of the Estate) and Standard 18 (Guardian of the Estate: Initial and Ongoing Responsibilities) to the extent the Guardian of the Person has been authorized by the court to manage the person's property.

Petitions the Court:

___Yes ___No ___N/A For limitation or termination of the guardianship when the person no longer meets the standard pursuant to which the guardianship was imposed.

OR

___Yes ___No ___N/A If there is an effective alternative to guardianship.

___Yes ___No ___N/A The guardian notifies the court when required and when there is any major changes in the person's life.

___Yes ___No ___N/A The guardian reports neglect and abuse issues to the appropriate authority.

NGA Standard 13—Guardian of the Person: Initial and Ongoing Responsibilities

__Yes __No __N/A Is there a case file for each person? Address ALL issues of the person that require immediate action:

__Yes __No __N/A During the initial meeting with the person was guardians' role and person's rights explained?

__Yes __No __N/A After the introduction meeting was an inventory of needs conducted to assess physical, social, educational, recreational needs and note person's preference?

__Yes __No __N/A Has an inventory of all Advanced Directives been created to include a living will, organ donation, contact persons?

__Yes __No __N/A Has a regular communication procedure been established between all individuals, organizations and service resources?

__Yes __No __N/A Has a written person centered guardianship plan been developed for short-term, as well as, long term goals that were both observed or included in the court order?

__Yes __No __N/A Was a financial review/audit completed on the person's financial assets and placed in the permanent records?

__Yes __No __N/A Has a personal budget been prepared?

__Yes __No __N/A On an ongoing basis does the guardian review/evaluate service provider plans and their implementation?

__Yes __No __N/A Does the guardian visit the person placed under a guardianship order monthly? If no, explain.

__Yes __No __N/A On an ongoing basis does the guardian examine all charts, notes, logs, evaluations, other documents at all sites that serve the person?

__Yes __No __N/A Does the guardian consider institutionalization placement only as a last option?

__Yes __No __N/A Does the guardian monitor and advocate for a person placed in a residential care facility?

NGA Standard 14—Decision Making About Medical Treatment

__Yes __No __N/A Does person have duly executed living will, durable power of attorney or oral declaration of intent?

___Yes ___No ___N/A Have person's wishes been requested for consideration in decision process?

___Yes ___No ___N/A Does guardian have a clear understanding of the medical issues and discussed the medical condition, proposed treatment options and preferences with the person placed under a guardianship order?

___Yes ___No ___N/A Has guardian received an independent second medical opinion when appropriate and discussed the person's preference with the physician providing the consultation?

___Yes ___No ___N/A Have legal/ethical considerations been identified and discussed with hospital ethics committee or legal counsel?

___Yes ___No ___N/A Has the guardian only denied medical treatment after doing a thorough review of person's history and determined what the person's preference would be if he/she was still competent?

___Yes ___No ___N/A Has the guardian sought court authorization for extraordinary procedures?

___Yes ___No ___N/A Has the guardian done everything he/she could to inform the person and get feedback from the person concerning medical treatment?

___Yes ___No ___N/A Has the guardian discussed palliative care with the person under guardianship order to determine preferences and values and in keeping with those wishes, incorporate palliative care in the health plan?

NGA Standard 15—Decision Making About Withholding and Withdrawal of Medical Treatment

In making this determination there shall in all cases be a presumption in favor of the continued treatment of the person.

___Yes ___No ___N/A Is there documentation of the person's prior expression or current preference regarding the withholding or withdrawal of medical treatment?

___Yes ___No ___N/A If the person's preferences are in conflict with the guardian's plan, has an ethics committee recommendation or court consideration been sought?

___Yes ___No ___N/A Has guardian completed a written statement fully explaining the reason the decision is contemplated; treatment options considered with each expected medical outcomes; the names of the individuals and their observations/opinions who's input was considered in the decision making process; and why the decision was made as it was?

___Yes ___No ___N/A Has the guardian completed research on the person's history to determine person's position on Withholding and Withdrawal of Medical Treatment was when the person as competent?

___Yes ___ No ___N/A If required by state law, has guardian secured proper court approval to withhold and/or withdraw medical treatment?

NGA Standard 16—Conflict of Interest: Ancillary and Support Services

___Yes ___No ___N/A Is the guardian program a free standing-entity?

___Yes ___No ___N/A Is the guardian independent from all service providers?

___Yes ___No ___N/A Does the guardian or guardian program provide any direct services to the person which could include housing, medical or legal services?

___Yes ___No ___N/A Has guardian employed his/her family or friends to provide services to the person?

___Yes ___No ___N/A Are service contracts awarded to providers based on their demonstrated capability to provide a quality service at a reasonable cost that will best meet the needs of the person?

___Yes ___No ___N/A Does the guardian receive or could receive any financial gain as a guardian besides the guardianship fees approved by the court?

___Yes ___ No ___N/A If compensated for other than fee-based services, has the guardian secured prior court approval for direct services rendered?

___Yes ___No ___N/A If guardian is an attorney and is addressing the legal needs of the person has this relationship been approved by the court?

___Yes ___No ___N/A Has the guardian informed the court and all involved parties of any potentially perceived, potential or actual conflict of interest?

___Yes ___No ___N/A Does the free-standing entity have a conflict of interest policy that complies with NGA Practice Standards?

NGA Standard 17—Duties of the Guardian of the Estate

Guardian of the Estate's sole responsibility is to manage all assets for the person's sole benefit.

___Yes ___No ___N/A Has the guardian prioritized the goals, needs and preference of the person and weighed the costs and benefits of the estate?

___Yes ___No ___N/A Has the guardian documented in the case file utilization of substituted judgment in managing the estate (considered current wishes, past practices, and reliable evidence of likely choices)?

___Yes ___No ___N/A If the guardian has not applied the substituted judgment standard, has the guardian documented in the case file utilization of the best interest standard in management of the estate (substantial harm would result or there is no reliable evidence of likely choices)?

___Yes ___No ___N/A Has the guardian documented in the case file efforts to assist and encourage the person to act on his/her behalf and to participate in financial decisions?

___Yes ___No ___N/A Has the guardian used reasonable efforts to provide oversight to any income and assets under the control of the person?

___Yes ___No ___N/A Is there a need for consultation with and delegation to additional personnel with appropriate expertise when managing the estate?

___Yes ___No ___N/A Has the guardian determined if a will or other pre-guardianship designations exist?

___Yes ___No ___N/A Has the guardian obtained copies of a will and other pre-guardianship designations (power of attorney, insurance beneficiary designations, payment of payment of death/transfer on death/joint tenancies) to determine how estate assets and property should be managed?

___Yes ___No ___N/A Does the guardian supervise all income and disbursements of the estate?

___Yes ___No ___N/A Does the guardian maintain accurate financial records and account fully for all estate assets?

___Yes ___No ___N/A Does the guardian employ prudent accounting and investment procedures when managing the estate assets?

___Yes ___No ___N/A Are the estate's assets maintained separately from all other individuals and their funds?

___Yes ___No ___N/A Has the guardian established procedures for making claims against others on behalf of the estate?

NGA Standard 18—Duties of the Guardian of the Estate: Initial and Ongoing Responsibilities

___Yes ___No ___N/A Has the guardian ascertained the income, assets, and liabilities of the estate?

___Yes ___No ___N/A During the initial meeting with the person was the guardians' role and person's rights explained?

___Yes ___No ___N/A Did the guardian obtain any previous or currently expressed wishes of the person?

___Yes ___No ___N/A After the introduction meeting was an inventory conducted of all assets for which the guardian is responsible listed by name, current value and location placed in the case file?

___Yes ___No ___N/A Has the guardian obtained all public and insurance benefits for which the person is eligible?

___Yes ___No ___N/A Does the guardian provide the opportunity for the person to manage the funds to the best of his or her ability?

___Yes ___No ___N/A Are all estate records complete, accurate and understandable?

___Yes ___No ___N/A Has the guardian developed and implemented a financial plan and budget for the management of income and assets that corresponds with the care plan for the person and aims to address the goals, needs and preferences of the person?

___Yes ___No ___N/A Does the financial plan emphasize a "person-centered philosophy"?

___Yes ___No ___N/A Has the guardian taken all steps necessary to obtain a bond sufficient to protect the estate?

___Yes ___No ___N/A Does the court accounting contain sufficient information to clearly describe all estate transactions?

___Yes	___No	___N/A	Is a written procedure in place for the disposition of the person's assets and the filing of appropriate final reports upon the termination of the guardianship or death of the person?
___Yes	___No	___N/A	Has a burial trust account and funeral arrangements been established?
___Yes	___No	___N/A	If the person resided in an institution-based residence does guardian monitor or manage the person's personal allowance?

NGA Standard 19—Property Management

Any change in the disposition of real or personal property must be in the best interest of the person.

___Yes	___No	___N/A	Has a plan been established for an independent or judicial review of any disposition of real or personal property?
___Yes	___No	___N/A	Has the person been asked about his or her desires relating to the property or whether there is an estate plan that must be considered or followed?
___Yes	___No	___N/A	Have the potential future benefits of the property been considered in making a decision to dispose of it?
___Yes	___No	___N/A	Has the condition of the property and the person's ability to maintain the property been compared to the liability and cost of maintaining the property?
___Yes	___No	___N/A	Has sufficient insurance coverage been secured for the property of the estate?

NGA Standard 20—Conflict of Interest: Estate, Financial, and Business Services

___Yes	___No	___N/A	Has the guardian avoided all conflicts of interest and self-dealing or the appearance of a conflict of interest and self-dealing?
___Yes	___No	___N/A	Are policies/regulations in place to monitor financial accounts relating to the possibility of co-mingling estate funds with personal funds?
___Yes	___No	___N/A	Where more than one person's funds are consolidated with another person's funds does the guardian maintain separate and complete accounting records for each person's funds?

___Yes	___No	___N/A	Where consolidated accounts are utilized are all fees and costs distributed equally or proportionately to each participating person's account?
___Yes	___No	___N/A	Is there a procedure established to approve/review all transactions of real or personal property to ensure that the guardian, his/her family, friends, agency staff or board member, etc., does not benefit in any manner from this activity?
___Yes	___No	___N/A	Has a continuous or periodic audit procedure been established to ensure that loans of any type are not made from estate funds or that estate funds are used for the benefit of someone other than the person?
___Yes	___No	___N/A	If income and assets are used to support or benefit other individuals, was prior approval obtained?
___Yes	___No	___N/A	If Yes, was a reasonable showing made that such support is consistent with the person's goals, needs and preference and will not substantially harm the estate?

NGA Standard 21—Termination and Limitation of the Guardianship/Conservatorship

___Yes	___No	___N/A	In the case of plenary guardianship, was a limited guardianship considered first?
___Yes	___No	___N/A	Has a procedure been established to identify under what circumstances will the guardianship seek to limit the scope of the responsibilities or by which a request would be made for terminating the guardianship?
___Yes	___No	___N/A	Has the guardian engaged in reasonable efforts to assist the person under guardianship to develop or regain the capacity to manage his or her personal and financial affairs?

NGA Standard 22—Guardianship Service Fees

___Yes	___No	___N/A	Is the fee reasonable for service provided while conserving the estate to the extent possible and service information accurately stated?
___Yes	___No	___N/A	Is the rate approved by the court?

__Yes __No __N/A Were fees collected in accordance with a court order?

__Yes __No __N/A If the estates will be exhausted is there a succession plan?

__Yes __No __N/A In the case of Medicaid beneficiaries, were fees sought consistent with the Standards?

NGA Standard 23—Management of Multiple Guardianship Cases

Based on an evaluation made indicating the complexity of decisions to be made, complexity of estate, and time spent.

__Yes __No __N/A Is caseload limit based on the ability to adequately support and protect the needs of each individual?

NGA Standard 24—Quality Assurance

Independent review (minimum every two years) of guardianship services provided includes:

__Yes __No __N/A Representative sample of case records review.

__Yes __No __N/A Review of agency policy and procedures.

__Yes __No __N/A Visit with the person under guardianship order.

__Yes __No __N/A Visit with direct service provider.

Independent review was conducted by one of the following systems:

__Yes __No __N/A Court monitoring system.

__Yes __No __N/A Independent peer.

__Yes __No __N/A CGC Master guardian.

NGA Standard 25—Sale or Purchase of a Guardianship Practice

__Yes __No __N/A Is guardianship practice a private, professional guardianship service?

When contemplating the sale of a guardianship practice or part of a practice, including "goodwill" are the following considered:

__Yes __No __N/A Persons are considered when selling the practice.

__Yes __No __N/A All guardianship responsibilities are met while the sale is pending.

__Yes __No __N/A Purchasers are qualified and are required to provide references.

__Yes __No __N/A The purchaser is engaged in serving or representing the person's interest.

___Yes ___No ___N/A Guardian provided written notice of the sale to the person, the court, and interested parties.

___Yes ___No ___N/A Guardian ad litem or a reviewer was requested to protect the person's interest.

___Yes ___No ___N/A All parties were responsible for the continuity of care and protection of the persons.

___Yes ___No ___N/A Are the guardianship service fees increased solely by the new owner to finance the purchase of the guardianship practice? (If yes, the Standards of Practice prohibit this.)

NGA Standards of Practice Checklist Summary

List the area where work is needed along with explanations and time frames.

Standard	Action Plan
1. Applicable Law	
2. Relationship to Court	
3. Relationship with Person	
4. Relationship with Family and Friends	
5. Relationship with Other Professionals and Service Providers.	
6. Informed Consent	
7. Standards for Decision-Making	

Standard	Action Plan
8. Least Restrictive Alternative	
9. Self-Determination of Person	
10. Duties regarding Diversity and Personal Preferences	
11. Confidentiality	
12. Duties of the Guardian of the Person	
13. Guardian of the Person: Initial and Ongoing Responsibilities	
14. Decision-Making about Medical Treatment	
15. Decision-Making about Withholding and Withdrawal of Medical Treatment	
16. Conflict of Interest: Ancillary and Support Services	
17. Duties of the Guardian of the Estate	

Standard	Action Plan
18. Duties of the Guardian of the Estate: Initial and Ongoing Responsibilities	
19. Property Management	
20. Conflict of Interest: Estate, Financial and Business Services	
21. Termination and Limitation of the Guardianship/Conservatorship	
22. Guardianship Service Fees	
23. Management of Multiple Guardianship Cases	
24. Quality Assurance	
25. Sale or Purchase of a Guardianship Practice	

GLOSSARY

In developing a set of principles and standards to be used on a national scope, it is necessary to review and consider the tremendous variety of terms that are currently in use throughout the country. Concerns with these differences and possible misinterpretation of principles and concepts led to the development of the terms and definitions used in this guide.

Advance directive A written instruction, such as a living will or durable power of attorney for health care, which guides care when an individual is terminally ill or incapacitated and unable to communicate his or her desires.

Advocate A person who assist, defends, pleads, or prosecutes for another.

Alleged incapacitated person Individual for whom a guardianship proceeding has been initiated. May also be called the **person at risk** or **respondent**.

Arm's length relationship A relationship between two agencies or organizations, or two divisions or departments within one agency, which ensures independent decision making on the part of both.

Attorney A person who practices law. May also be called **legal counsel** or **lawyer**.

Attorney for the alleged incapacitated person An attorney who represents the alleged incapacitated person. Such attorney represents the expressed wishes of the alleged incapacitated person.

Best interest The course of action that maximizes what is best for a person and that includes consideration of the least intrusive, most normalizing, and least restrictive course of action possible given the needs of the person.

Capacity Legal qualification, competency, power, or fitness. Ability to understand the nature of the effects of one's acts. State definitions may vary.

Clerk of court A court officer responsible for filing papers, issuing process, and keeping records of court proceedings as generally specified by rule or statue.

Competent A basic or minimal ability to do something; qualify esp. to testify, competence of a witness.

Conflict of interest Situations in which an individual may receive financial or material gain or business advantage from a decision made on behalf of another. Situations, which create a public perception of a conflict of interest, should be handled in the same manner as situations in which an actual conflict of interest exists.

Conservator A person or entity appointed by a court with the authority to make some or all financial decisions on behalf of an individual the court determines needs assistance in making such decisions.

Corporate guardian A corporation that is named as guardian for an individual and may receive compensation in its role as guardian with court approval. Corporate guardians may include banks, trust departments, for-profit entities, and nonprofit entities.

Court An arm of the government, belonging to the judicial department, whose function is the application of the laws to controversies brought before it and the public administration of justice. Depending on the jurisdiction, the court hearing guardianship cases may be in the probate division or a general jurisdiction court.

Court order A legal document issued by the court and signed by a judge. Examples include a letter of guardianship; spelling out directions for the care of the person and the estate and authorization or denial of a request of action.

Court-required report A report that the guardian is required by statute or court order to submit to the court relative to the guardianship.

Court visitor A person appointed by the court to provide the court with information concerning a person or guardian. May also be called a **monitor** or **investigator**.

Decisional capacity The ability to understand and appreciate the nature and consequences of a decision and to reach and communicate an informed decision in the matter.

Dementia A general term for a decline in memory or other thinking skills severe enough to interfere with daily life. Alzheimer's disease is one form of dementia.

Designation of guardian A formal means of nominating a guardian before a guardian is needed.

Direct services These services include medical and nursing care, care/case management and case coordination, speech therapy, occupational therapy, physical therapy, psychological therapy, counseling, residential services, legal representation, job training, and other similar services.

Disabled person An adult found by the court to be lacking sufficient understanding or capacity to make or communicate responsible decisions concerning the care of her/her person or financial affairs. See also **person under guardianship**.

Emergency/temporary guardian A guardian whose authority is temporary and usually only appointed in an emergency.

Estate Both real and personal, tangible, and intangible, and includes anything that may be the subject of ownership.

Extraordinary medical measures Includes abortion, removal of life support, sterilization, experimental treatment, and other controversial medical issues.

Family guardian An individual who is appointed as guardian for a person to whom he or she is related by blood or marriage. In most cases when there is a willing and able family member who has no conflict with the alleged incapacitated person, the court prefers to appoint the family member as guardian. On court approval, a family guardian may receive reasonable compensation for time and expenses relating to care of the person.

Federal fiduciary An individual, agency, or organization appointed by the Veteran's Administration to manage a person's veteran's benefits.

Fiduciary An individual, agency, or organization that has agreed to undertake for another a special obligation of trust and confidence, having the duty to act primarily for another's benefit and subject to the standard of care imposed by law or contract.

Foreign guardian A guardian appointed in another state or jurisdiction.

Freestanding entity An agency or organization that is independent from all other agencies or organizations.

Functional assessment A diagnostic tool that measures the overall well-being of an individual and provides a picture of how well the person is able to function in a variety of multidimensional situations.

Guardian An individual or organization named by order of the court to exercise any or all powers and rights over the person and/or the estate of an individual. The term includes conservators and certified private or public fiduciaries. All guardians are accountable to the court.

Guardian ad litem A person appointed by the court to make an impartial inquiry into a situation and report to the Court.

Guardian of the estate A person who possesses any or all powers and rights with regard to the property of the individual.

Guardian of the person A guardian who possesses any or all powers and rights granted by the court with regard to the personal affairs of the individual.

Incapacitated person A person a court has determined to be unable to make personal and/or financial decisions in whole or in part and needs the assistance of a guardian.

Incapacity A person's inability to make and then act upon personal and/or property decisions on his or her own behalf. State definitions may vary.

Informed consent A person's agreement to allow something to happen, made with knowledge of risks involved and the alternatives. A patient's knowing choice about a medical treatment or procedure, made after a physician or other healthcare provider discloses whatever information a reasonable prudent provider within the medical community would give to a patient regarding the risks involved in the proposed treatment or procedure.

Interested person Individuals who, according to state statute, have a right to notice regarding a guardianship cause of action. This may include parents, siblings, spouse, and residential provider.

Intellectual disability This disability, which begins before the age of 18, is characterized by significant limitations in both intellectual functioning and in everyday social and practical skills.

Least intrusive A mechanism, course of action, or situation which allows the person the greatest opportunity for autonomy with a minimum of intervention.

Least restrictive alternative A mechanism, course of action, or environment that allows the person to live, learn, and work in a setting that places as few limits as possible on the person's rights and personal freedoms as is appropriate to meet the needs of the person.

Letters of office Formal document issued by the court containing or attesting the grant of some power authority or right. May also be called **letters of guardianship**.

Limited guardian A guardian appointed by the court to exercise the legal rights and powers specifically designated by a court order entered after the court has found that the person lacks capacity to do some, but not all, of the tasks necessary to care for his or her person or property, or after the person voluntarily petitions for appointment of a limited guardian. A limited guardian may possess fewer than all of the legal rights and powers of a plenary guardian. May also be called a **partial guardian**.

National Certified Guardian An individual who has met the qualifications established by the Center for Guardianship Certification.

National Master Guardian An individual who has met the qualifications established by the Center for Guardianship Certification.

Palliative care Specialized medical care for people with serious illnesses. It focuses on providing patients with relief from the symptoms and stress of the illness, as well as pain management. The goal is to improve the quality of life for both the patient and the family.

Person-centered planning A family of approaches designed to guide change in a person's life. This type of planning is carried out in alliance with the person, their family and friends, and is grounded in demonstrating respect for the dignity of all involved. The approaches seek to discover and understand the unique characteristics of the person so he or she has positive control over the life he or she desires and finds satisfying; is recognized and valued for contributions to the community; and is supported in a web of relationships within his or her community.

Person under guardianship (or simply, **"person"**) A person the court has determined requires assistance in making some or all decisions, and for whom the court has appointed a guardian. Synonyms include **person subject to guardianship, conservatee, disabled person, incapacitated person, protected person**, or **ward**.

Personal representative A person appointed by the court to manage the assets and liabilities of an intestate decedent (one who dies without having written a will). An executor is a person named by the testator (a person who has made a will) to carry out the provisions in the testator's will. May also be called **executor** or **administrator**.

Petition A formal, written request presented to a court or other official body, such as the document filed to initiate the process to determine a disability and appoint a guardian.

Plenary guardian A person who is appointed by the court to exercise all delegable legal rights and powers of the person after the court has found the person lacks the capacity to perform all of the tasks necessary to care for his or her person or property.

POLST POLST stands for Physician Orders for Life Sustaining Treatment. Typically a state-prescribed POLST form is prepared for very sick patients with multiple chronic conditions. It records in detail the decisions made by the patient and puts those decisions into medical orders to be followed in a medical crisis. Some states may identify these orders as MOST or POST.

Pre-need guardian A guardian who is formally nominated before a guardian is needed.

Professional guardian An individual, who is not related to the person by blood or marriage and who, with court approval, may receive compensation in his or her role as guardian. Usually acts as guardian for two or more individuals.

Prudent investor rule An investment standard in which all investments are considered as part of an overall portfolio rather than individually. Under most circumstances, the person's assets must be diversified. The prudent investor is obligated to spread portfolio investments across asset classes and potentially across global markets to both enhance performance and reduce risk.

Psychotropic medications Any medication prescribed for the management of behavior.

Public guardian A guardian appointed by the court, who is deemed to be an officer of the court. This person or agency may be appointed to guardianship over many incapacitated persons. The appointee may be paid for services from public funds or from assets of the incapacitated person, if such funds are available. Usually a public guardian is appointed when no one else is willing or able to act as guardian.

Representative payee An individual, agency, or organization named by a governmental agency to receive government benefits on behalf of, and for the benefit of, the beneficiary entitled to such benefits.

Respondent The person against whom a guardianship petition has been initiated.

Self-determination A doctrine that states that the actions of a person are determined by that person. It is free choice of one's acts without external force.

Social services Services provided to meet social needs, including provisions for public benefits, case management, money management services, adult protective services, companion services, and other similar services.

Standby guardian A person, agency, or organization whose appointment as guardian becomes effective without further proceedings immediately upon the death, incapacity, resignation, temporary absence, or unavailability of the initially appointed guardian.

Substituted judgment The principle of decision making that requires implementation of the course of action which comports with the individual person's or beneficiary's known wishes expressed before incapacity or prior to the appointment of the guardian or representative payee, provided the individual was once capable of developing views relevant to the matter at issue and reliable evidence of these views remains.

Successor guardian A guardian who is appointed to act upon the death or resignation of a previous guardian.

Surety bond Obligation of a guarantor to pay a second party upon default by a third party in the performance the third party owes to the second party.

Trustee One who, having legal title to property, holds it in trust for the benefit of another and owes a fiduciary duty to that beneficiary. Generally, a trustee's duties are to protect and preserve the trust property, and to ensure that it is employed solely for the beneficiary in accordance with the directions contained in the trust instrument.

Volunteer guardian A person who is not related to the person by blood or marriage and who does not receive any compensation in the role as guardian. The guardian may receive reimbursement of expenses or a minimum stipend with court approval.

WEBSITES

AARP: www.aarp.org

Alzheimer's Association: www.alz.org

American Bar Association Commission on Law and Aging: www.americanbar.org/aging

American Bar Association Section on Real Property, Trust and Estate Law: www.americanbar/groups/real_property_trust_estate

American College of Trust and Estate Counsel: www.actec.org

The ARC: www.thearc.org

Center for Elders and the Courts: www.eldersandcourts.org

Center for Guardianship Certification: www.guardianshipcert.org

Hospice Foundation of America: www.hospicefoundation.org

National Academy of Elder Law Attorneys: www.naela.org

National Center on Elder Abuse: www.ncea.acl.gov

National College of Probate Judges: www.ncpj.org

National Disability Rights Network: www.ndrn.org

National Guardianship Association: www.guardianship.org

National Hospice and Palliative Care Organization: www.nhpco.org